MW01257487

You Took the Kids

WHERE?

Adventuring While
Your Children Are Young

Doug Woodward

with **Trish Severin,**
Canyon, Rivers, Forest, Autumn, David and Cricket Woodward

Foreword by Patch Adams

HeadwatersPublishing.com

Headwaters Publishing
412 Thunder Creek
Franklin, NC 28734
whitewater6@gmail.com
HeadwatersPublishing.com

First Edition: 2017

Library of Congress Cataloging-in-Publication Data

Woodward, Doug, 1936 –

You Took the Kids Where? Adventuring While Your Children Are Young / by Doug Woodward.—1st ed.

320 p; 109 photos; 21.5 cm

ISBN 978-0-9779314-3-9 (trade paperback)

1. Child rearing 2. Parenting 3. Homeschooling 4. Adventure travel
5. Alternative lifestyles 6. Self-reliant living

D.D. Classification 649.1

Library of Congress Control Number 2017904036

To Trish

*My wife, friend and fellow dreamer, who through her vision,
planning and enthusiasm, made possible the adventures
that have been the unique education of our children.*

Contents

Foreword   vii

Preface   1

Rolling Through Adventure   3

Into the Unknown   19

A Storm to Remember   31

Surviving Hell's Half Mile   39

Life on the Mountain   49

Journeys that Intersect   55

What About Schooling?   61

Riding a Westward Wind   77

Journey of the Heart   99

Choose Love, Not Fear   115

Wilderness Challenges   131

The Far North   135

A Wilder Place   159

Lives We Had Never Imagined   173

Could Anyone Do That?   193

Who Are We Now?   199

    Autumn   201

    Forest   211

    Rivers   219

    Canyon   225

    David   237

    Cricket   243

    Trish — Dreamer of Possibilities   251

    Trish and Doug   255

Reprise   257

Appendix

    Making It Happen —
    A Nod to the How of Adventuring with Children   259

    The Backcountry Adventure   261

    The Trail   265

    The River   271

    The Byway   283

    Learning from the World   291

Acknowledgements   299

Foreword

After offering a lecture at North Carolina's Guilford College more than a decade ago, a student named Autumn Woodward approached me and we chatted for perhaps ten minutes. It was quickly evident that the two of us shared similar values and had even had some of the same experiences, despite the difference in our ages. Autumn is the daughter of Doug Woodward, author of this book and, over the years, continues to be one of my closest personal friends.

In my now 49 years of practicing medicine, I am still amazed by the stories that Doug's family has shared with me. His family has one of the healthiest relationships with each other that I have ever known. Rarely have I heard from others about the absolute bliss that comes with the authentic love parents might share with their children, and how this love can produce compassionate and effective adults.

I have lectured in more than 80 countries, and have asked social workers and psychologists how many families they believe have a loving and healthy relationship. Rarely have they estimated more than about one in five.

From the very beginning, Doug and his wife, Trish, included their children as participants in adventure, whether that meant taking them into wild country or introducing them to folks with very different lifestyles. Hiking, bicycling, canoeing, kayaking and camping were a way of life for them. At a time when most children suffer from what might be thought of as "nature deficit disorder," Trish and Doug's family were one with nature. Nature appears even in the works of art and poetry they produce.

All children need to develop a similar deep concern for, and an ethic to work toward the protection of nature. If we introduce children to nature as a nurturing friend, rather than something to be dominated, then many of the conditions thought to be mental illness would surely disappear.

Wow, I now think to myself, how thoughtful of Trish and Doug to want their children to travel and live in foreign lands. I'm sure most U.S. citizens would be frightened and unprepared to travel in countries where there has been political upheaval, extensive poverty and customs different from our own. Tourists tend to travel in their own comfortable styles. Imagine the understanding possible if travelers stepped out of their comfort zone, lived with those living in poverty, ate their food, and became familiar with the surrounding community.

When I was reading this book, I felt I was reading a romantic fairy tale. These were not trips from brochure packages. The parents planned and the whole family jumped in, trusting to their own experience and the loving kindness of friends as yet unmet. We — those of us working toward a vision of healthcare for all, regardless of resources — have wonderfully benefited from this family's experiences because two of their children have traveled with me on our clowning mission trips.

There is no magic wand that can transform all families into ones like Trish and Doug's. Their family is quite unique. Their adventures did not happen because they were rich. They were able to travel because of their conviction and determination toward healthy parenting. And healthy parenting is connected to a healthy future for all of us.

With a deep hunger to understand our unhealthy society, we must acknowledge the flaws in our public schools. We should triple the salary of teachers, give them autonomy over lessons, remove the grading scale, and gloriously feed the individual students' interests, watching them grow into caring, creative, cooperative, loving and thoughtful adults. The Woodward family has four beautiful children. All have homeschooled, each of them excelled in college, and each has grown into the kind of adult that you would appreciate having as your friend.

In a splendid supplement at the end of the book, Doug outlines in extensive detail how he and Trish raised their children close to nature and simpler cultures. Maybe in a generic way, I feel this book says, this may be the only way. If you and your family have a desire to do the same, then go for it!

If you want healthy children, if you have concern for your children, then work toward the intention of offering sweet parental love with excited devotion to the opportunity of exposing your children to the intimacy of nature. Feel the bliss of learning, and the brotherhood-sisterhood of all people. Since the first day I spoke with Autumn, I've been enchanted by her stories of family. They give me strength.

— Patch Adams, MD

You Took the Kids Where?

Preface

Very early in our parenting years, in fact even before our children had been born, my wife, Trish, and I realized that we wanted to provide the opportunity for our kids to choose paths for their own lives that might be quite different from those that our prevailing society would choose.

We would, as best we were able, give just enough advice for our children to make intelligent decisions, yet be free to step outside the conformity of our social order and explore, to paraphrase Robert Frost, "the path less traveled," ultimately determining their own direction.

There were two tenets that Trish and I had found to be true in our own lives. That time spent in the wilds of nature can nourish and renew our spirits, and that living daily life with those who have few material possessions can be an awakening experience.

And, connected to those two was another pair — that we have a responsibility to engage with the suffering of humanity in a meaningful way; and that we must protect our wild country, not just for its beauty, but because it makes possible our very existence on this planet. It was only natural, at least for us, that we would share such values and experiences with our children.

Almost from birth, the kids were introduced to the world in that way. From the time that, as infants, they could hold up their own heads, each child began to savor the sights and fragrances of alpine flowers at the edge of a massive glacier, or the shy but friendly smile of a Quechua child peeking around the corner of her hut.

What started as an ever-evolving plan for childhood adventure and education quickly became a way of life for our family. We all learned new lessons. We looked forward to each new chapter. The children grew. Trish and I had to run to keep up.

Now, as our youngest has passed the age which our society accepts as adulthood, we can look back over the growing years of all the children with a broad look at what these experiences have meant to each child. This book spans more than three decades of unique family life, touching on the reasons we chose this path, and where each sibling is now.

Your children will not necessarily select the experiences which our own children have chosen — but each child can open her eyes to the many possibilities that exist, a discovery of her own distinctive abilities, and the way in which these can be shared as a gift to all whom she will encounter.

As important as community and friendships are, there is another world beyond the familiar everyday routine of school, sports and the activities which so much of our present society considers necessary for filling a child's schedule. It is a world which offers the seeds and tools for understanding those whose lives are quite different from our own. One which presents lessons in self-evaluation and an ability to walk easily on this earth, whether it be on the streets of Kathmandu or in the forests of the Amazon.

And for those who would follow some of these same paths, the last portion of this book contains the "nuts and bolts" of how we traveled as a family, both in wilderness country and cultures different from our own, with hints for creating enthusiasm for the adventure among the young ones, as well as lists of the basics necessary for each type of experience.

May your own path and adventures give you and your children the journey about which you have dreamed.

Rolling Through Adventure

"Hey, would ye like a cup of tea?"

After ten kilometers without a sign of human habitation, I'm startled as a voice from the wild landscape between the narrow road and pounding sea grabs my attention like a hand on the shoulder. But I quickly brake, bringing my bike and child trailer to a stop. The bush, as Australians and New Zealanders refer to wild country, is dark, seemingly impenetrable, but my son Forest and I soon pick out a gate and the smiling figure behind it.

Smithy, well-known throughout New Zealand's South Island, is the soul of hospitality. His friendly horse and dog standing beside him, he invites us to stop and share our story. With the feeling of a beautiful encounter not quite fulfilled, I tell him that we must decline, since half of our family — my wife, Trish, and daughter, Autumn — somehow missed his call and are churning down the coastal road ahead of us.

Historian and longtime resident of the Island's west coast, Smithy has an insatiable curiosity for the tales of travelers that pass his gate. As quickly as I can — but not nearly doing justice to the experience — I tell him that Trish and I have been biking the South Island for ten weeks, carrying our camping gear, clothing and food, as well as Autumn (4½) and Forest (nearly two).

Thanking Smithy for his warm offer, Forest and I bid him goodbye and turn to the task of overtaking Trish and Autumn as we head south once more. Two kilometers later, we find the girls waiting at the top of one of the west coast's many steep hills. Go back for a second chance with Smithy? No, we regretfully decide — not on the bicycles.

Very likely, this will be the longest family biking experience of our lives. Eleven weeks on the road and countless mountain climbs and hair-raising descents later, we find our muscles hardened to deal with whatever the terrain may offer. Having ridden through days of pounding rain and high winds as the Marlborough Straits — the strip of ocean between the North and South islands — were being lashed by a slow-moving cyclone, our kids had little idea of Mom and Dad's ordeal as they sat snug in their child trailer behind my bike. On mild weather days, Autumn and Forest would ride behind one of us and Trish and I would alternate carrying each of them.

Doug and Forest on New Zealand's west coast road, South Island.

We had planned this adventure for most of the past year, thinking that we would bike for a month, rent a car for a month, and select a beautiful spot to stay put for a month, enjoying the best of both islands. My, how dreams can change!

Although the sale of our small rafting business on the Nantahala River in North Carolina paid for airfares for the four of us, we remained on a very tight budget. Despite camping and visiting occasional Servas[1] hosts, we quickly found that without an auto-

mobile industry in New Zealand, the cost of automobile rental —
or purchase, should we wish to buy and sell before leaving —
was prohibitively high. Scratch the motorized month.

Then, after the first month on bikes, deciding that our bodies
could do it at ages 37 and 51, Trish and I said to each other, "Let's
stay with this mode of travel for the entire three months." We did.
And what's more, we chose to stay on the South Island the whole
time since there was so much more to experience, and so many
had already reached out to offer us their friendship. In many
ways, the island was like a small town.

Biking the "most beautiful road" in Zealand, on the north coast of the South
Island, through clouds and heavy rain, with no view at all!

But days when the kids were confined to the child trailer could
be brutal. This meant that we were riding through steady rain,
Trish and I wondering whether the water running down our
bodies was more from leaky rain gear or the sweat of exertion.

But the boredom inside the trailer could be intense, as small
voices behind me cut through the rain.

[1] Servas is an organization of travelers and hosts, committed to furthering world
peace through understanding between cultures. A normal stay is two nights,
which can make for delightful visits. We host at home and occasionally journey
as Servas travelers. For more information, see servas.org

"What can I do, Dad?"

"Read one of your books."

"I've already looked at them four times."

"Eat your raisin snack — make it last."

"It's gone. And Forest just pooped in his diaper. It stinks in here."

"We'll stop soon and I can change it."

"Forest ate some pennies."

"What! How did he do that?"

"I gave them to him, to see if he would."

"Jeez, Autumn, he's not a vending machine!"

For two days, whenever I change his diaper, I dissect Forest's poop looking for the small change. And sure enough, I find the pennies, burnished to a bright luster by stomach acid. Since Autumn can't remember how many she gave him, we're never quite sure if the count is correct.

We pray for sunshine.

~ ~ ~

Let's pause on that New Zealand road for a moment and examine our rationale for including our young ones in such an adventure.

There are reasons why children should have encounters which take them — and their parents — out of the comfort zone. One of the most important of these is discovery — uncovering the passion within each child for unique learning experiences that reach far beyond the walls of the traditional classroom. Learning that your everyday world of home is but a tiny part of the vast network of lives on this planet, lives that are perhaps quite different from our own, yet just as dependent on the environment which we all share. Beginning to understand these differences, rather than walling ourselves away in some tiny "safe zone."

Whenever possible, we take time out for pure fun. Here, Autumn and Forest explore a cave on our canoe trip up the coast of Abel Tasman National Park, New Zealand. March, 1988

But infants, toddlers and children who haven't even been exposed to formal learning yet? Absolutely. What better time to offer unusual learning opportunities to a fresh young mind, before the rigidity of society creates beliefs and prejudices that are so hard to overcome.

Later, I'll share suggestions for bringing extraordinary family experiences into your own life, but more importantly, as you travel with us on these pages, I hope you'll understand our reasons for embarking on such adventures. I'm not saying that these reasons and these adventures must be yours, but simply that they have worked very well for our family.

There are many important areas that have had an impact on our children's self-confidence and growth. Two of these stand out —

acquiring the skills to be at home in the wilderness, as well as developing a heart connection with it; and understanding the lives of those who live in cultures quite different from our own. In both of these areas — and they are often mingled together — our family has tried to be present with open minds, open hearts and the desire to learn from new friends and new experiences, as well as from the natural world around us.

And we found, no matter how much we think we might already know as parents, that there is so much more to learn from others, and the experience will have as much value for us as it will for our children. There may be opportunities to share our own skills, but primarily we found that we should all be there simply as appreciative, open-minded friends.

~ ~ ~

Although I speak largely of family travel adventures in these pages, it is obvious that most of our time will be spent much closer to home and that many defining opportunities will occur there. Seize them!

Is there a creek close by for your kids to adopt? Learn about water quality, how to test it, who to contact to correct pollution or erosion problems. Make friends with the "critters" who call this waterway or wetland their home.

Is there a student from a different country who is struggling with his language skills? His writing? Be his friend and share your ideas and know-how as a parent or a buddy. Include him in fun family activities.

Is there a nursing home near you? If so, there are older folks, each with a unique story, just longing to hear the voice of a child or to share a hug.

Does your local government need reminding of issues that require attention — environmental responsibility, social justice, the opportunity to create a park or greenway? Well-presented letters and testimony from young folks can have far more impact than the words of adults.

Over the years, our family — as each child became old enough to understand the action needed, and to participate — created groups that had not previously existed. *Families Learning Together*, a statewide North Carolina network of homeschooling families. *Ed-venturous Learning Families*, a similar group serving western North Carolina. *Voices for Peace*, an activist network advocating peaceful alternatives to war. A citizens' network to publicize the consequences of drilling for gas by fracking and the effect on our quality of life.

~ ~ ~

And these children. Your children. Those little beings that you have helped enter this world and who now trust you implicitly — what qualities do you want to see nurtured and strengthened as they grow into their own vision and away from yours? What lessons will you have modeled for them, what compass will you have given them? The earliest years are so important in setting an example and defining the values that give meaning to their lives.

Too late comes all too soon.

Making ourselves part of their lives in a very real, hands-on way has paid intangible dividends to each child's character and to the way in which she or he chooses to engage the world. Thoughts blossom. Questions flow. We don't have all the answers, but we do try to stimulate curiosity, encouraging them to keep open minds so as to appreciate quality in the lives of all whom they encounter.

~ ~ ~

Now that you have a glimpse of why we are here, let's hop back on our bikes and see what's around the next bend of that New Zealand road.

During our first week of riding, we have a tough 30-mile day climbing over Mt. Michael, are chased and drenched by three thunderstorms, and finally take refuge in the health-food store and restaurant in Fairlie.

Seeing that we are a family on bikes, and aware of the dark clouds building for yet another storm, Elizabeth, the proprietor, invites us to be her guests for the night in the caravan behind her home. She must work until 8pm, but we are to go on and make ourselves comfortable in her caravan — we would call it a mobile home in the U.S. — until she arrives. We cook dinner for her — a spinach-tofu quiche — as the ever-present rain plays a tune on her roof.

~ ~ ~

Have you ever encountered a "person of mystery," with whom you instantly identify, but realize certain parts of his or her persona will remain forever hidden? Such was the case when we met Mick Hutchins on a stormy morning near the small town of Wanaka, astride his mountain bike, his face barely visible within his dark woolen hooded cloak. A kind face with serious gray eyes, a receding hairline, but immediately alive with adventure, humor and tales untold.

He is "Strider" himself, straight out of Tolkien's "Ring" escapades, on a two-wheeled journey that would intersect our own at this propitious moment. We had been gifted by our first New Zealand hosts with a chance to stay in their small A-frame vacation cabin close to Wanaka. After a few words with Mick, we invite him to escape the cold wet elements and share the warm shelter. He graciously accepts.

Mick has tales that hold us spellbound. He has been a college professor at Oxford, but left to become a gypsy, traveling by horse and wagon in England for several years, has also sailed extensively, climbed, tramped, kayaked — you name it! We talk until midnight, then step outside to breathe the clearing air and absorb the starry night sky and Southern Cross.

Mick is very interested in our child trailer and we agree to try to get it to him before leaving. He and his wife, Sharon, biked down the west coast with their two-year-old daughter until Sharon found out she was pregnant again and returned home. Home for Mick and Sharon is a community of 28 persons living "Amish-style" in the bush near the Heapy Track.

As we part ways, I pick up my camera but Mick stops me with a gesture. "No photo. Just remember me in your heart," he says. And we will. His journey is unpredictable. He can't tell us where he'll be, but probably somewhere on the South Island. "But how will we get the child trailer to you?" I ask. "You'll find me," is the enigmatic reply.

~ ~ ~

When we arrived in Christchurch, we had deposited our trip funds in the Bank of New Zealand and carried with us a list of the BNZ branches. Our longest day yet of biking tallies 54 miles in foul weather, including a gale with enough muscle to blow me and the kids in my attached child trailer right off the road not once, but twice. Exhausted, we roll into the small town of Owaka, which boasted a BNZ branch as well as the last store for many miles.

The rain eases late in the afternoon, as we pull up in front of the Owaka store. Selection is unbelievably bleak — no cereal, no whole-grain bread, no crackers, no powdered milk, no, no, no — we finally buy a loaf of white bread and a few other "make-do's."

Well, maybe we can find groceries somewhere once we withdraw more cash, though it seems unlikely. Now comes the big shock. The Owaka Branch of BNZ is only open one day a week, and we've arrived on the day after. With empty pockets and hungry stomachs, we're suddenly finding the limitations of bicycle travel. But on we go, looking for the farm cottage which will be one of our few splurges of the trip — that is, if we can figure out how to pay for it.

Trish and Forest on one of the many gravel roads on the South Island.

Another half-mile down the road, we make a left and shortly encounter hosts June and Murray Stratford. June is out painting the mailbox and Murray is on his way to help his neighbor with the haying. Our cottage is about half a mile away, a spacious three-bedroom farmhouse, actually. We're delighted with the space after weeks of camping! June and Murray have about 1,700 acres of land, with 8,000 to 9,000 sheep, a good many red deer, and cattle too. Our cottage is surrounded by flowers, and a child's swing delights Autumn and Forest.

June, on hearing of how we struck out at both store and bank in Owaka, says, "Never mind the bank. Give me your emergency U.S. travelers check — we'll estimate the exchange rate — and I'll cash it. Make out a grocery list, I'll ring up the postman in Balclutha, and he'll bring the groceries with the mail tomorrow."

Sure enough, the postman, having shopped on his own time and money — until we could reimburse him — comes delivering the mail with two bags of groceries marked "Woodward" on his back seat. We could have hugged him — and did hug June.

Forest and Autumn enjoy the swing at June and Murray's sheep farm, having been confined to the child trailer for one of our longest days.

~ ~ ~

"Oh shit, we're going down!" the voice inside my head screams. Autumn is in the child seat behind me, rather than in the safer enclosure of the trailer, and I've let our speed be determined by gravity on this downhill run. Even the main roads are gravel in the southern section of the South Island but, for the most part, quite rideable on mountain bikes. On this one, however, the steepness has contributed to the deep accumulation of stone near the bottom of the hill.

I hit the heavy gravel and lose it, going into a long painful slide on the road. Autumn bites her lip, but is mainly scared. I've got a bloody left leg and arm, and my back feels a bit wrenched. The bike seems to be OK once the handlebars are straightened.

"I knew you were going too fast," Trish admonishes. Will I be too stiff to ride tomorrow, I wonder?

Actually, I feel great in the morning! Calendula cream and arnica have done a quick healing job. Even the deep gravel cuts seem well on their way to being healed. The fact that we're in good shape from the daily riding has likely contributed also.

~ ~ ~

The skeleton in the Takaka cave.

"Is that a real person?"whispers a small voice beside me as Autumn and I stare at the skeleton lying on the floor of the cave.

"Yes it is — or was. They think he fell through the sinkhole in the field above us sometime in the last century," I reply.

"Well, why didn't they bury him?"

"They probably figure he's already buried down here." I can tell that my sensitive daughter is replaying the scene in her mind.

Trying to distract her a bit, I offer, "Have you seen the other bones over here?"

"Was it a bird?"

"Indeed it was — a Moa. The Moa could grow to a height of twelve feet, twice as tall as a human, but it had no wings. It is believed that the Maori people, who lived here long before the English came, hunted the birds until they became extinct about 600 years ago." Before Autumn can plumb the shallows of my limited South Pacific knowledge, we emerge from the Takaka Hill cave and rejoin Trish and Forest.

We're still resting our muscles from the morning climb, one of the most grueling of the whole adventure. For over three hours, pedal stroke after pedal stroke, consuming every snack and drop of water within reach, we've inched our way up Takaka Hill. Now comes the reward. The downhill run into the valley of Golden Bay. But first, check those brakes — pads, cables and adjusters.

Slowly and steadily, switchback after switchback, we descend toward the brilliant sunlight and soothing greens of Golden Bay. At last we level out among the sunny emerald fields where we'll spend the next several days relaxing, visiting hidden waterfalls and picnicking by the gushing waters of Pupu Springs.

A million people live on New Zealand's South Island. But, as has been said many times, it truly is a "small town." By the end of our eleven weeks, we had begun to run into folks we had seen earlier. It did not take many enquiries before a rider replied, "Oh yes. Mick. He's in Queenstown, working with the Forest Service." We put the child trailer on a train with that barebones address, and after we returned to North Carolina, there came a note from Mick, thanking us and assuring us that it had arrived.

~ ~ ~

"I know they are the same ones — we saw them at the dinosaur slide at Wanaka Park." We overhear the family in the Picton grocery store whispering among themselves, and realize that we are the subject of their conversation as they steal glances in our direction. Once again we appreciate the close community on the South Island of New Zealand. But on the other hand, a family with two small children traveling by bicycle does stand out. One more, of many circles, has finally closed.

By now, we've found that our paths have re-crossed the journeys of many others as we share time with residents and travelers alike.

"Did ye bike through that cyclone?"

"What did ye think of that hell-bent descent from Arthur's Pass? Do ye have any brakes left?"

"Ah, you traded your bikes for a canoe for a week and camped up the coast of Abel Tasman? Good on ye!!"

Time and again, those were the words that would bring a smile to our faces and warm our hearts during this family adventure. They were, in effect, the most heart-felt of blessings that could be bestowed by a New Zealander.

"Good On Ye!!" indeed.

~ ~ ~

And, of course, you may be saying, "We can't do that. We're not like you. We don't think it's possible." Physically, it's absolutely possible. I was 51 years old when we biked those eleven weeks in New Zealand, and that was only the beginning of our family adventures. Most parents of small children will be much younger and in better shape.

But what about my job? What about the money it takes to do these things? Those of us in the United States live in a culture that worships "more" and "newer." We are conditioned to think that more money and the latest, most up-to-date "things" will bring us the freedom we want. All that does is increase the fear that we are going to lose it or someone will take it from us.

Thus the alarm systems, gated communities, financial advisors and huge insurance policies which make prisoners of us, and make it harder, if not impossible, to leave home or shift lifestyles. But the most important aspect of life — love, friendships and warm experiences — cannot be lost or stolen. They can be shared or given away, and will still always be with you.

Sure, both Trish and I left our jobs years ago with modest savings, some helpful events occurring along the way. But our income has always been at the low end of the scale. When we planned a lengthy adventure, it meant belt-tightening before, during, and after, shopping for bargain airfares if we were leaving the country, camping out wherever we went, and using the cheapest local transportation if we weren't on our own bicycles.

Not all jobs are full-time, of course, such as teaching with summers off or working seasonally as a chef. I knew a welder who simply lived to run rivers. He worked hard approximately six months of the year, and had fabulous canoeing adventures until he needed to work again. There are many avenues to attaining that golden prize called "time."

I also mention a consideration which is probably obvious to the reader, but should be pointed out anyway. When we moved from our home in the Atlanta area to the southern Appalachians, our property tax rate became less than a tenth of what it had formerly been.

But even though there was no turning back for us, Trish and I did not jump off the cliff blindly. We had enough resources saved to carry us forward for a year or more, depending upon how frugally we lived. Both of us had worked traditional jobs (engineering and teaching) for a number of years, but during that time — including the years before we met — we had each taken every opportunity to maximize our adventure time, whether it was paid or unpaid leave from our jobs. We knew well that it was "time" — and having the choice to use it as we chose — that was the most valuable aspect of our lives.

Team Gemini (Trish and Forest) in New Zealand circa 1988. "Mamma crushing the hills, me crushing the raisin boxes. So much love for Mom, today and every day; the mover-shaker and dance-party rager, community giver and green-thumb digger, dreamweaver and higher-good believer … cheers to all the mothers." — Forest's words, 28 years after that New Zealand adventure.

Into the Unknown

Before exploring our family's earliest years, let's look at a moment in time when all four younger children have come into our lives. Our youngest son, Canyon Sage, is four years old. He and I are sitting behind our home, listening to the soothing sound of water tumbling down the mountain, discussing some of the projects underway around our place. Trying to compare the freedom of our family with the constraints of other families that he knows, he asks how I'm able to be present when so many other parents are not.

I explain that it was not always so; that both Mom and I worked traditional jobs for many years — that Mom enjoyed teaching and I felt the satisfaction of completing an engineering project. He is silent as his young mind digests the "then and now." Finally, he looks at me with his most serious face, having pictured how I might have left engineering.

"Did you escape while they were sleeping?"

Indeed! I could not have summed it up any better.

~ ~ ~

When Trish and I met, we were both backpacking on Cumberland, a wilderness island off the Georgia coast, accessible only by boat. Our first date, a week after returning to the mainland, was a whitewater canoe and kayak run of the Yellow River near Atlanta. Obviously, we shared a love of outdoor adventure. It was the glue in our relationship and would continue to define our life together.

Two years and many rivers later, Trish and I were married before a handful of family and friends in the woods surrounding our Lilburn home north of Atlanta. As an adjunct to our regular jobs, the two of us had started teaching outdoor skills to children through Headwaters, a small company we had created. Our weekends were filled with these programs, taking us to many of the same places we enjoyed on our own, but now giving us the opportunity to share our passion for wild places with eager kids.

Headwaters grew, as many children that we worked with caught our own enthusiasm for connecting with nature on the rivers and trails of Georgia and North Carolina. Trish and I were a team of two, with very different personalities, but working well together in teaching outdoor skills or planning logistics.

We might take a whole classroom to Cumberland Island for a week to integrate camping proficiency with the knowledge of what is happening in the island's ecological zones, from the ocean to the marsh on the mainland side. A highlight would be seining in the surf or marsh, always bound to turn up a scary critter or two, including the common stingray.

Other weekends would find us camping in the mountains of North Carolina, rafting half a dozen students down the whitewater of the Nantahala River, then teaching them kayaking basics on Fontana Lake.

But our lives were about to undergo a more radical change. Trish was teaching at Galloway, a private school in Atlanta; and I was working as an engineer for Western Electric in Norcross, Georgia. Our outdoor excursions would almost always find us camping in the mountains of north Georgia or North Carolina.

"What if we didn't just go there, but actually lived there?" was a question Trish loved to pose.

Well, what if we did? Gulp! Leaving my engineering work and a reliable income gave me a sinking feeling in the pit of my stomach. But Trish had no qualms whatsoever about parting with her teaching job.

"You've always told me that time is worth so much more than money — now's our chance to find out!"

"But if I worked three more years as an engineer, my age and service would qualify me for an early retirement package. We'd be so much better off financially."

"Nope. That's an excuse. Let's do it *now*!"

My time with Trish found us enjoying wild places together, a passion that would shape the destiny of our children yet to come.

Trish, being a risk-taker, and always a catalyst for change, felt strongly drawn away from the city, to an area where our daily lives would be surrounded by beauty. For the first time in my own life, without a clear vision of how we would make it all work, I took her hand and agreed to do it.

We began to search the North Carolina mountains for land or rentals and tally up what we might have if we liquidated our house and land in Georgia. We put the house up for sale, and it sold — at our asking price. We gave notice to our employers and jumped into the unknown.

~ ~ ~

Now we were on a schedule. But in fact, we decided to ignore that schedule for two weeks and just kick back with a road trip north to contemplate what we had done. Camping, hiking and canoeing through the Smokies and the Blue Ridge, we followed the back roads all the way to my mother's farm in Maryland. The feeling of freedom was huge — the anxiety slight. The anchors had been cut free.

There was no looking back, only forward. We found an old North Carolina farmhouse hidden away in a mountain hollow and offered the owners $200/month to rent it. They accepted, but wanted to see our marriage license first, since Trish's and my last names are different. No unmarried hippies gonna be doin' their thing in our farmhouse!

The little farmhouse we rented in the North Carolina mountains — drafty and cold, but home to us when Autumn was born.

Friends helped us load the rented truck for a do-it-yourself moving job and on a snowy, muddy November day we took possession of our new abode, surrounded by mist and mooing cows.

We had taken that first step — a big one, and maybe right into a cow-pie — with no assurance that it was the right one. But getting closer to the wild places we loved wasn't the only reason for our moving to the mountains. Long ago, we had both come to believe that time — our own time — was worth so much more than money. Now we would have a chance to prove the truth of it ... or not. Maybe, just maybe, if we simplified enough, and continued to teach outdoor skills to children, we could make it without having to check in at a job every morning.

It certainly wasn't paradise that we had found. Even though our private little valley gave us large doses of solitude, Trish didn't know how long she could stand the ever-present morning mist that closed us in, or the chorus of mooing cows at the bedroom window. Gradually these feelings were replaced by her appreciation of the simplicity that our lives had embraced. Having grown up on a farm, the cows didn't bother me as much. I was just delighted not to be milking them twice a day!

But right now we still had questions that kept coming to the forefront of our minds. Was our timing right? Should I have worked longer as an engineer, rather than retiring early without the perks? Did we have enough funds to make it ... make it to what? By liquidating everything, we could live for a while on what we had, or ... we could buy a piece of land, build our own home and make it for a shorter time.

And what about land? We had searched the mountains for "just the right piece" from The Tennessee-North Carolina border east nearly to Asheville. And if we found that perfect piece, how perfect would the price be? Well, sometimes fate puts the pitch right over home plate, but you'd better be looking if you're going to hit it out of the park.

The walk from our rented haven in the cow pasture to our mailbox was half a mile and we usually walked it for exercise and the beauty of emerging up into the broader valley. One day the mail was late and I found myself pacing the shoulder of the road as rain began to fall. An older neighbor who was also waiting invited me to hop into his Blazer and escape the weather.

I did just that, and soon heard Orville — for that was his name — fuming over his property tax bill, which had arrived the day before. At that time, Macon County only adjusted property values every eight years, making the change rather noticeable.

"Why, I'd sell my place for half what the county says it's worth," Orville growled.

"Are you really trying to sell?" I asked. When the answer came back affirmative, I followed up with, "Where is your place?"

As it turned out, his land adjoined the farm where we were renting, though we had never ventured up his private road before. He lived in a funky little place he had built himself, with mountain bedrock protruding ten feet into the living space. Rain water and copperheads also arrived via the same slab of rock.

But … there were redeeming qualities. His cabin was south-facing, giving solar options. There was a commanding view of the Little Tennessee River Valley and the more distant mountains of Standing Indian. Gravity water would provide independence from pump and well. And most impressive of all, the creek tumbled down the mountain in a 70-foot falls, right behind the house.

As you may have guessed, we bought Orville's place. Yes, at half the county's assessment, cabin included, an unheard-of deal. Trish and I later looked at each other and I had to admit, "This would never have happened if I had worked three more years to qualify for early retirement, not to mention being three years behind on our life's plans."

And our lives were changing. By the time we became the owners of Sliding Falls Ranch — Orville's mountainside spot, named for a wandering cow that had met her demise in a plunge over the waterfall — we knew that Trish was pregnant. The nesting instinct of an expectant mother calmed her restlessness, and she took a keen interest in our home-to-be.

Time became more critical as we rushed to tear down Orville's leaky cabin, and I would spend the hours after dinner under the roof that was left, working up house designs on my drawing board while whip-poor-wills just outside sang the evening into night.

Certain basics were required. Even before we purchased Orville's land and cabin, we knew that we must have a south-facing home-site in order to incorporate passive solar into our design, which would, in turn, cut the quantity of needed firewood in half.

High-quality water, without the chlorination or fluoridation of metropolitan water, was a necessity. An added bonus would be gravity flow from the mountain, delivering the water independently of electrical power. A relatively flat area below our home, where I would clear existing forest, would soon become our organic garden.

With the design complete, we shifted into an even higher gear. A local sawmill cut our beams to order and delivered them. We left the stonework and slab from Orville's cabin and built up from there. My 18-year-old son David helped with the heavy part of construction on weekends, mixing concrete for footings and being part of the four-man crews that worked the foundation beams into place.

David lived for six months in an old cabin above our waterfall, finishing high school and working for a local surveyor when he wasn't helping us. By this time, both he and his sister had the experience of two Alaskan river trips, as well as many local outdoor adventures.

His sister Cricket, 20, living in Colorado Springs, was halfway through her biology degree at Colorado College when we made the leap to the North Carolina mountains. She had fallen in love with the West, and often joined her younger siblings in our family adventures on the rivers and trails of Colorado, Utah and Washington.

A 300 lb, 8"x12" beam is readied for placement by David, Doug and two friends as our mountain home takes shape.

As our North Carolina summer turned to fall in a blaze of red maple and golden hickory, our daughter Autumn was born with a full moon bathing the mountains in silver light. On September 23, the same day that I had appeared on earth, Autumn became the best-loved birthday present I have ever received!

Our routine now became more rigorous. I would work during the day on our building project, mixing and carrying concrete or mortar for footings and stonework, fitting rocks into place, and leveling the whole structure for new beams.

Trish would nurse Autumn day and night, trying to catch an afternoon nap. One of us — depending on our energy — would cook dinner and then I would dance Autumn to sleep in my arms to a recording of lively dulcimer music.

That winter was one of the coldest on record for western North Carolina as temperatures in our little valley dropped to sixteen below zero for two consecutive nights. Even with the wood stove blazing, our water pipes froze and I lay under the kitchen counter at 3 a.m., heating the copper pipes with a propane torch to break loose the ice. Trish bundled up three-month old Autumn and headed for Christmas in Atlanta with her family, while I stayed in the farmhouse to maintain heat.

We replaced the ancient woodstove in our rented house with an airtight Papa Bear to cut down on drafts and to raise the inside comfort level. We would "preheat" wool clothing — particularly Autumn's — in the morning by placing each piece on the surface of the hot woodstove for a few seconds before transferring that welcome warmth to a waiting body. We also quickly learned never to put any clothing article made with synthetic fiber on the stove!

Even as the frigid weather descended on our valley, Trish continued to take walks with Autumn, feeling much more a part of our choice to make our home here. Her journal notes reflect this mood:

The other day we sat on the rock — our hobbit spot — and watched the birds dash in and out of the trees, sunlight casting shadows through the meadows. A beautiful sunset — pink filtering through the clouds. I feel so alert to everything outdoors — so much loveliness right in this valley — opening my eyes — seeing it. The mountains are home now — my restlessness seems gone. I feel so content and happy with our land, and living in this area.

Meanwhile, work on our new place progressed through all kinds of foul winter weather. Two unemployed seasonal raft guides from Nantahala Outdoor Center helped me in the rush to get the house dried in. Neither was an experienced carpenter, but their help was invaluable. We were tied in with climbing lines or short tethers as we slid sheets of plywood into place to form the roof sheathing, a sleet storm doing its best to discourage us.

Windows were tricky, particularly on a wet or icy ladder, as they had to be set in their openings from the outside, balancing twelve feet above the ground. We were partial to wood — board and batten Cyprus on the exterior, tongue and groove pine on interior ceilings, walls and floor. It was at this point that the reality of my measuring, cutting and installing every one of these boards set in.

"Get help!" Trish urged. And we did. We hired a trio of experienced carpenters, that team saving us another year of rent in the old farmhouse, which nearly equaled the cost of their salaries. By June of 1984, we were able to move from the farmhouse into our own self-designed and self-built home, even though much work remained to be done.

Though I had never had the experience of building a complete house before, I had carried through projects of plumbing, wiring, and carpentry in existing homes in which I had lived. When I worked as a Georgia Tech co-op student for General Elevator in Baltimore, I designed a number of penthouse to basement layouts for elevator installations. What couldn't be figured out on the spot in our new home — and almost everything could — often could be answered with a quick question to a professional.

Moving from the farmhouse to our new home made the timeline a bit easier since we could now finish projects on our own schedule, as dollars became available. But the biggest lesson we would learn from this transitional experience — and we knew it well beforehand — was that, in order to live a frugal lifestyle that would continue to keep our time choices available, we must do every task possible ourselves, rather than paying someone else to perform it.

While in the farmhouse, Trish and I had bought an aging 15-passenger van and taught a few more Headwaters courses with our Atlanta base of students. But with Autumn's birth and the geographical distance from our students, it became impractical to continue.

To provide a small amount of income, I had completed a degree in surveying from Southwestern Community College

(Southwestern Tech at the time) and did a number of plat drawings for a local surveyor, all prior to the advent of computer-generated plats.

Our savings — depleted significantly by the house building — became a larger piece of the puzzle. Nevertheless, keeping track of our spending by means of a tight budget was the prime factor in our financial survival.

Orville, from whom we had purchased the property, was now in his mid-eighties. He delighted in visiting the newly emerging vision to keep up with our progress, often bringing his friends to view the changes, which included a bedroom view of our waterfall and a panoramic vista of the Little Tennessee River Valley.

Trish would walk up the mountain almost daily with Autumn bundled under her down jacket to see the progress we were making. And as the house took shape, she would make suggestions for change, many of which were incorporated into the design.

"How about a high window over the stove and another above the front door?"

"And if we eliminated the vaulted ceiling back here, we could add a small upstairs room — it could be my office!"

Designing and building our own home to blend in with its natural surroundings was a time-consuming task, yet we still managed to plan and enjoy short outdoor adventures in our surrounding mountains. When an irresistible winter day of sunshine and blue skies burst upon us, we would often bundle Autumn up and hike to the top of Wesser Bald, or perhaps bike the 19-mile Burningtown loop as she enjoyed a seat behind us, or even carefully buckle her into a small life jacket for an afternoon paddle down the Little Tennessee River.

Sometimes, we traveled a bit farther.

Nearly hidden on the mountainside, our new abode was to eventually become home and classroom to our family of six.

A Storm to Remember

A Storm to Remember takes place in central British Columbia, in September of 1985, when Autumn was not quite two years old. A ten-day circuit of lakes, rivers and portages becomes an odyssey of challenge and reward.

~ ~ ~

I should have expected it, I suppose. This was the fascinating woman whose canoe routinely disappeared around the bend while all the other paddlers were still getting their gear together. The same woman who had called me for our first date — on a whitewater river. The one who had survived the loss of both of our kayaks on the Tatshenshini River, deep in Yukon Territory, and come back for more. Trish. My partner and soul-mate.

Even so, despite my knowing her passion for sudden changes in course, my Gemini wife caught me by surprise.

Our daughter Autumn was not quite two, but Trish and I had been introducing her to the wild country of rivers and trails ever since she could hold her head up alone. We had planned a backpacking trip in the Olympics of Washington state, Trish's home territory. Our flight from Atlanta to Seattle had been reserved weeks ahead, our trail days planned, camping gear fine-tuned, and backpacks ready to check on board. Two days before we left, the latest issue of one of our favorite outdoor magazines arrived in the mail.

"Hey, look at this article!" Trish handed me the magazine.

"Beautiful country," I replied as I continued to run through my checklist of tasks needing completion before we left. "I'll read it later."

"No! Read it now. It's a ten-day canoe trip in British Columbia. We could do it instead of this backpacking trip."

My jaw dropped. "You're kidding, I hope. Everything is set for the Olympic Peninsula and we're leaving the day after tomorrow." But it was Trish, her mind going a mile a minute in a new direction. My gut began to get a familiar, uneasy feeling. I knew she wasn't kidding.

"Look, it could be a great trip. We fly to Seattle as planned, rent a car and drive the 400 miles north to the Bowron Lakes. I'll check on renting a canoe there, and if it's a go, we start switching our camping gear from backpacks to waterproof river bags. I'll call Ross and see if he and Karen can go with us." Ross Brown, a long-time friend of Trish's, was a NOLS (National Outdoor Leadership School) instructor and he and his wife, Karen, had a sea kayak of their own.

Sure, I thought. Karen is six months pregnant with their first child and we're giving them a whole two days of notice to get it together. Not a snowball's chance in hell they could go.

I was dead wrong, of course.

~ ~ ~

Three days later, on September 3, the five of us are sacked out in a tiny cabin in British Columbia's Caribou Range, resting for our morning departure. Rain pours down on the cedar shake roof all night long, punctuated by canon-shots of thunder.

By morning the downpour has subsided, but dark, ominous clouds hang low. Karen and Ross are packing gear into the center hatch of their tandem sea kayak while we load our sleek eighteen-foot rented lake canoe, carefully fastening Autumn's life jacket, but leaving her seat loose in case of a capsize.

By the time we depart on our seventy-two-mile circuit of lakes, rivers and portages, the sun has broken through and the clouds are scudding for the horizon. We quickly cross the north end of Bowron Lake and unload for the mile-and-a-half portage to Kibbee Lake. Portages with a wee one are a challenge, as Trish takes a load while Autumn toddles behind, then stays with her at the end of the portage trail. I return to hoist the canoe onto my shoulders for the second trip.

The paddle across Kibbee is only a smooth, sunny mile and goes quickly — the next grunting portage, a mile and a quarter. How about wheels for the canoe next time? Our bodies are feeling the effects of our overloaded foot travel, and we make camp after paddling less than two miles on Indianpoint Lake.

Ah, the dawn sunshine was simply a seductress. Morning rain catches us in the middle of cooking a pancake breakfast. We pack up a wet camp, Indianpoint Lake glides under us much too soon and we find ourselves at the third portage trail, a mile trek to the head of Isaac Lake. The rain follows us as we make the multiple, muscle-numbing foot-trips once more. The toughest portages are now behind us and we're looking at thirty miles of open water ahead.

But Mother Nature says, "Not so fast, my friends." A wind is rising and whipping the surface of the lake into a frenzy. Steady, hard rain continues to fall. Soaked right through our rain gear and badly chilled despite the strenuous exercise, we hug the north shore to avoid the waves and finally give it up seven miles into Isaac. We set up camp at the mouth of Wolverine Creek, which we see rising significantly in the hours following our arrival.

As the rain soaks our camp, the five of us huddle around a small fire, partially protected by a tarp, trying to absorb a bit of warmth. We each hold a piece of Autumn's clothing over the flames on a stick, attempting to dry her limited wardrobe as best we can.

All night, and throughout the next day, the rain and wind continue. Isaac Lake resembles a storm-tossed ocean, the wind blowing the tops right out of the five-foot waves. One of our two days' emergency food supplies is eaten as we use the time to discuss alternative plans beside the fire. Karen and Ross will wait out the weather and paddle on, even if we don't. They figure that they can make up a portion of their lost time in the sea kayak, by far the fastest craft on the lake.

Autumn sleeps in the pouring rain while the rest of us hurry to set up camp.

Shortage of food is not yet a concern, but could become one. For us, the most pressing question is whether we can keep Autumn dry and comfortable. Even being as careful as we can, her fleece clothing is getting wet right through her full rain suit. At this point, with only about a sixth of the trip distance behind us, it would make sense for us to reverse our direction if we need to escape the weather. The discouraging part of that plan is the fact that we would have to retrace almost four portage miles with our canoe and supplies. The four remaining portages are relatively short compared to what we've already done.

At dusk, the storm takes a more ominous turn. The wind velocity has increased noticeably and has a howling voice of its own. We can hear "tongues" of wind racing down the ridges above us with a force that is flattening trees in their path. They fall like dominoes, often ten or twelve in series, one crash rapidly followed by another. Becoming increasingly uneasy, we count hundreds of crashes in an hour.

Autumn watches as Trish serves dinner prior to the storm.

"Do you think any of the trees here in our camp could come down?" a concerned Trish asks.

I try to reassure her. "I don't think so. The dead trees have been cut out near our camp, the ones most likely to fall."

I rig our lightweight tarp over the tent and rain fly, trying to add a third layer of protection from the foul weather. Autumn is the only sound sleeper in our tent tonight, trusting her parents implicitly, as only a two-year-old can do. Trish and I toss fitfully, listening to the trees crashing as the wind roars down Wolverine Creek from the north.

In Edgar Allen Poe style, the storm chooses the black of night to hurl its worst at us. We hear it coming, but the warning offers no escape. As the violent river of wind envelopes our tiny camp, a tree trunk explodes no more than thirty feet from our tent. I reach for Trish, and together we try to shield Autumn as we wait out the longest four seconds of our lives. With the impact, our tent jumps and the earth moves beneath us as if it were liquid. I shine a light out of the tent door and see nothing but branches.

"We're out of here!" shouts Trish as she scoops Autumn into her arms and bolts for the edge of the lake. I follow as quickly as I can gather the tent and sleeping bags into a bundle that can be carried. A sixty-foot Douglas fir lies between our tent and the spot where Karen and Ross were sleeping, pinning one edge of our tarp to the ground. I shiver as I think of the probable results had the tree fallen a degree or two to either side of the spot it actually hit.

The other four are already on the rocky beach, Autumn no doubt wondering what in the world her parents are doing, dragging her around in the middle of the night like this. I re-erect our tent at the wind-swept edge of the lake, we climb in to escape the ever-present rain, trying to find depressions between the rocks for our hips and shoulders.

Morning arrives at last and we drag our aching bodies out of the tent once more. The rain has stopped, but a stiff wind — no comparison to last night's blow — is still kicking up whitecaps on the lake. We inspect the fallen tree we so narrowly escaped and breathe a silent thanks. The campfire is resurrected and a few pieces of Autumn's clothing are dried completely. After a long discussion and some initial hesitation, Trish and I decide to paddle on, keeping our small group together.

A stiff wind, and the possibility of a mid-lake capsize, dictate that we hug the eastern shore of Isaac Lake. We're physically drained from the previous night and camp only nine miles farther down Isaac, at the mouth of an unnamed creek. The wind is easing up, the sky beginning to clear, but the temperature is plummeting. We spend a frigid night snuggled together.

Discussing alternative plans as the rain continues.

Nevertheless, we greet the next day with energy, paddle the remaining fifteen miles of Isaac Lake, run the exit chute into the Isaac River, and make two relatively short portages. The halfway point of our trip finds us setting up camp at a beautiful spot on the edge of the river. Sunshine streams down through the treetops to turn the river mist into a luminous cloud.

It is now autumn in the North Country. There is no doubt whatsoever as the air is calm, the sun pleasantly warm and the nights have a sharp bite to them. We glide smoothly along Lanezi, Sandy and the Spectacle Lakes, snow-capped peaks rising from the Mowdish, and Quesnel Ranges. A string of mergansers dives, one by one, from a log as we pass. Sand beaches are a delightful playground for Autumn. She stuffs herself with blueberries from the bushes that surround our camps. Loons serenade us far into the evening. We are paid back in exquisite currency for the pounding we took at Wolverine Creek.

Doug, Autumn and Trish prepare for the final day of paddling on British Columbia's Bowron Lakes.

Surviving Hell's Half Mile

The canyon of the Green, high above Rippling Brook, the campsite that captured us on every subsequent Green River trip.

The story that follows is based on my journal account of our first family trip on the Gates of Lodore section of the Green River (Colorado/Utah) in 1991. Autumn was 8, Forest 5 and Rivers 2. Canyon was not yet born. Besides Trish and myself, my oldest daughter, Cricket, 28, was part of the crew. The Green became a regular adventure for us, always in the low-use season after mid-September, which, despite chilly weather sometimes mixed with snow, permitted us six nights on the river rather than three.

On our next trip, in 1993, Canyon, at seven months of age, became one of the youngest to run the Green.

But ... let's look at our first fall adventure on this historic river, the hesitation beforehand, and the confidence that grew as we negotiated rapid after rapid.

~ ~ ~

We make camp by the Green River to begin thinking whitewater and to await my daughter Cricket's arrival. On our way by the NPS River Office, we find out that the flow is 1300 to 1400 cfs, not 800 cfs as we were led to believe — we're not yet sure whether this is good or bad news. Cricket, my oldest, surprises us and zips into camp in time for dinner after driving eleven hours from Santa Fe with only a brief rest. It's great to have her here so soon.

As the campground gradually begins to fill, three men pull into a site near us and begin unpacking river bags. Trish goes over to talk and I join them about twenty minutes later just in time to catch tales of heavy water, plowing into unavoidable rocks, and getting thrown out of the raft — they've just finished the trip we plan to do.

About an hour later, Trish approaches me in the dark and says, "There is no way the kids and I are going to run that stretch of river! Those men are experienced — both on the Green and other rivers — and they had a lot of problems. One even fell out of the raft when they hit a rock in an unnamed rapid!"

I think to myself, experience and skill do not necessarily equate, and I counter with, "Two factors I noticed which indicate questionable judgment — they were pulling firewood on an inner tube tied to their raft (a loss of steerage) and they had quite a supply of beer on the river (including a good bit left over)."

Even so, Mom's apprehension has spilled over to the kids and they all express negative thoughts about running the river. I don't sleep well that night, and the thought of one of the kids being tossed out in a large rapid haunts my dreams.

Sunday morning and it's our launch day. I flag down the ranger circling through camp and ask him about the river flow.

"Oh, it's running 1800 cfs — always does this time of year — Flaming Gorge has to release enough to take care of irrigation rights downstream." One more opinion to put in the grinder, as the water level goes up another notch.

After discussing our options, including splitting up (some on, some off the river), we decide to head for Gates of Lodore launch site, talk to the ranger there, and evaluate the situation again. We gas up in Maybell and make Lodore by noon. A group from Boulder is preparing for their launch the following day. They assure us that the kids can walk around any difficult rapids and that the higher water level should help by washing out some of the rockier stretches.

More than that, their experience — from many trips down this section of the Green — has a calming effect on the kids and the beauty of the red rock canyon we're about to enter beckons to us all.

Our consensus is to go ahead as planned, all of us launching together here at Lodore, but a certain tension still remains. Despite many long family trips in the wilderness, and years of paddling whitewater rivers, none of us have run the Green before, and this will be our first experience with guiding a heavily loaded raft on a multi-day river trip. How well will our kayaking and canoeing skills transfer to rafting?

Dark clouds seem to boil right out of the towering red-walled chasm that forms Gates of Lodore and we're drenched in a gusty rain squall as we scramble to assemble the raft and frame, and to pack and load gear.

Carrying a load of gear to strap into the raft, I slip and fall prostrate in the mud. A few minutes later, Rivers does the same and ends up sitting in the river — not a happy prospect for a 2½ year-old when dry clothing is limited. Trish and I explode at each other and embarrass ourselves in front of the Boulder folks.

We've used up far too much of the afternoon but at last we're ready. Despite — or perhaps because of — our frayed nerves, the Boulder folks have stayed close, lending a hand here and there. One of them — Philip — catches me alone and slips a small animal bone into my palm.

"Keep this with you on the river — don't lose it — no one will swim, you'll enjoy the river and the weather will smile."

I thank him and tuck the bone safely into my paddling shorts, where it will remain for the rest of the trip. The weather has already begun to smile as the late afternoon sun paints warm colors on the canyon walls. But with October only a day away, the daylight will not last long and we must be off. I hand my camera to RW, one of the Boulder oarsmen, and he takes a picture of us — afloat at last!

The put-in fades into the distance as the oars dip and we slide silently toward the mouth of the canyon. We'll soon find out how well we've planned our first week-long family rafting trip. Hours of adding to, or discarding items from, our equipment lists have brought us to this moment of truth. Trish has wrestled with menus and food lists — will the grocers in Vernal have what we've planned? — while I've tried to cover as many scenarios as possible should we lose or break any of our equipment.

There will be no rapids this afternoon as we pull into shore an hour later, now well into the canyon. We set our camp not far from the ruins of the old Wade & Curtis cabin; dinner is finished in the dark. As soon as dishes are done, we turn in for sleep — tomorrow will be a demanding day and the one just past has had its own share of stress.

Forest takes the oars in a calm section of the Green River as Cricket waits a turn (1998).

Morning is chilly, but the myriad faces of early light draw our eyes to the beauty above and around us. In the low-use season — which we're now in — river-runners are allowed to burn driftwood and the warmth from the morning fire feels great. A large pan is used to contain the fire; and ashes, as well as dishwater, are strained and carried out. All human waste is taken with us as well.

We notice that the release from Flaming Gorge is not constant and the river has dropped about six inches overnight. But it's now on the rise and by mid-morning, as we take to the current again, we're riding a crest. I feel good about the way the raft has handled so far, but today I know the raft and oarsman will be put to the test.

Our first challenge will be Upper Disaster Falls, where the wooden boat, No-Name, was broken in two and lost on John Wesley Powell's 1869 exploratory expedition. A scant four miles below our camp, we carefully watch for the islands and steep canyon wall on river left that will mark our approach to this rapid. Even so, I almost put the raft right into it and only a grinding minute of back-ferrying pulls us away from the brink.

On land once more, the six of us follow the shore for the next half-mile to Lower Disaster Falls, scouting the continuous rapid as best we can, our view being partially blocked by an island. Autumn, Forest and Rivers strip to their skin and enjoy playing in an eddy at a sandy beach while Cricket and I make our way back to the raft. As we approach the main chute of Upper Disaster, our velocity increases, position is perfect, and the broad hole is punched with little difficulty. The next half-mile demands a number of moves, but there is plenty of time for each, and Cricket and I decide that 1800 cfs must be an ideal water level for this rapid. We spin happily into the kids' eddy. In retrospect, I decide, I would certainly run it with all hands aboard.

A quick lunch and it's on to Triplet Falls. When you're in the right place in this rapid it looks easy, but it takes a strong ferry left to get there after S-turning through the upper part. If you miss the exit route, the main current will take you right into two room-sized boulders, almost assuring a flip or pin. The kids walk around, but I feel confident enough that I would take them through next time. Our run is uneventful.

The walking and scouting has slowed us down and shadows are creeping into the canyon. Hell's Half Mile still stands between us and camp, two miles away. Another ten minutes on the river and we can hear the roar of the rapid. Scouting this one is mandatory. One look at the entrance and I motion the kids to walk — Hell's will have to wait until they are a good bit older.

A string of rocks — looking for all the world like huge teeth — blocks most of the river as it begins to drop steeply. An opening left of center marks the only possible route at this level, as half the flow seems to be rushing into this gap. Within thirty feet, the river pours over a six-foot drop and into a violent back curl. The hole must be avoided with a quick and strong ferry to the right just after passing the entrance rocks.

I set up for the right-hand move. The first stroke is good, but the second catches an underwater rock and pops the oar off of its pin. Before I can recover, the raft slants down the right shoulder of the drop, spins 180 degrees and hangs on the big boulder that the main tongue is pouring over. Cricket instinctively jumps to the right place and bounces the raft free as I jam the oar back into place. The rest of the run is full of challenges, too, but none that match the first drop in excitement!

The "walk-around" almost matches the rapid in difficulty as the billy-goat trail soars high above the river with a sheer drop to the water's edge. Cricket ties off the raft and we both scramble back up the trail to help Trish with the kids. All in the raft again, we now relax and look forward to the Rippling Brook campsite, twenty minutes ahead.

Camp is made at the lower site, a beautiful shaded area with a pebble beach and rocks convenient for sitting. Autumn, Forest and Rivers are immediately off to explore shallow caves near the sparkling stream that comes skipping out from between the western canyon walls. In retrospect, Rippling Brook became our favorite site — calling us back in the years that would follow.

Autumn and Forest take turns building, lighting and tending the morning and evening fires, a favorite task. Our dinners are basic — lentils and rice, tortillas, spaghetti and the like — and most welcome. There are no leftovers! The sky is ablaze with constellations and paints the canyon with its own soft light through the clear night air.

The kids share the chores appropriate to their ages and observe how gear is secured in the raft, how the raft itself is rigged for rowing; and begin to absorb a feel for how the raft must be positioned for a successful run of each rapid — skills that will serve them well in years to come.

Mornings are nippy (in the 40s), but quickly the sun brings its warmth to the day. From Rippling Brook, we slide into the fun rapids of Whirlpool Canyon, passing the impressive Steamboat Rock to arrive at Echo Park for lunch. The Yampa River joins the Green River now in the most spacious area we've seen since entering Gates of Lodore.

Our friends from Boulder catch us here, we exchange a few river experiences and they decide to eat lunch while they row. We suspect they want to make sure of first campsite choice at Jones Hole, where they'll spend three nights. We relax for an hour, fill water jugs and take to the river again. The next five miles are soon behind us as we pass the Boulder folks making camp at Jones Hole One. Jones Hole Three is our choice and we set up amid the luxury of picnic tables and outhouse. (Outhouses have since been removed and all waste is now carried out with each rafting party.)

We spend two nights at this friendly area, enjoying dips in the crystal-clear creek and hikes up the canyon to appreciate colorful vistas and pictographs from Anasazi times. Cricket and her lizard-catcher — a loop of dental floss with a slip knot at the end of an old retractable fishing pole — are a hit with the kids as several individuals are looped and identified, then returned to their rocks. A gopher snake is taking in the morning sun, and as it senses our presence withdraws backward into its hole. Two garter snakes make it a three-snake day.

We get to know our neighbors better, too — they've made the Green River a tradition, usually planning two trips a year. Todd, RW, Bill and Philip have been running rivers for a good while, Kim has friends at the Nantahala Outdoor Center near our home in North Carolina, and Lois refers to herself as an aging hippie.

On the second night, they plan a Mexican party, complete with a piñata containing play money, fake jewels and real condoms! Cricket and I arrive in time for the campfire, which is a fun round of stories, songs and jokes. Philip is just starting an animated take-off of one of Robert Service's poems as we find a spot near the crackling flames. Lois interjects lively comments and emphasis throughout.

Cricket lends her captivating voice to several songs, tells an off-color joke that has the group almost rolling into the fire, and I contribute my rendition of the Eddystone Light. After learning that all the children are mine — plus one not on the trip — a few condoms are passed in my direction!

With only seven miles to our next camp, we take our time packing and loading next morning, making a late start on the river. We pay for it, as a fierce wind comes up after lunch and at times actually blows us upriver. Swinging the bow downriver for stronger leverage, Cricket and I take turns pitting our best strokes against the wind.

At last we make camp at Island Park, a more exposed location than any we have camped at yet. The wind does not abate, blowing sand into everything in its path and adding another dimension to the chores of setting up tents and cooking dinner. Sunset is beautiful, but we sleep fitfully as the tents at times seem close to taking flight.

Our last day on the river dawns calm and we try for an early start to avoid afternoon headwinds in Split Mountain Canyon and to give Cricket more time for her drive to Santa Fe. The rapids in Split Mountain seem no more intimidating than on our evening run last summer — a short, full-moon trip which had only whetted our appetite for more of the Green. Perhaps at a higher water level the rapids have more bite. Even SOB, with its many moves, goes by smoothly.

The bone Philip had given me at the put-in still remains in my pocket and the river experience has gone just as he predicted.

Apparently, the spirit of that small animal still watches over the Canyon of Lodore!

Coming ashore at Jones Holes on the Green River on a later trip in September of 1998. Rear, left to right: Forest, Trish, Doug, Canyon. Front: Rivers and Autumn.

Life On The Mountain

Our goal in coming to the mountains of western North Carolina was to take complete control of our own time, even though it meant living on a fraction of our former income. We knew that we would be doing the tasks ourselves — including building our own home — that others would pay someone else to perform. Four children later, we were not only surviving, but thriving.

For those not familiar with the topography and climate of North Carolina, I would emphasize that the Southern Appalachians in the western part of the state not only enjoy four seasons, but can experience winters similar to New England. Before the decade of the eighties had come to a close, we would see two 30-inch snows, both dumped on us in successive years during the month of April!

In the winter of '93, several snows had already made access over our half-mile of gravel road difficult, but still possible. With Trish entering her ninth month of pregnancy in mid-January, we kept a close ear to the weather forecasts. Would our midwife be able to make the hour-and-a-half drive from Asheville, or were we taking too big a chance on a home birth?

As it turned out, Trish's labor started at two in the morning, we called our midwife, Jade, at 4am and Canyon greeted us late in the afternoon of a beautifully clear winter day, an underwater birth in Trish's favorite haven — our comfy old claw-foot bathtub! A few weeks later, we were hit by the Blizzard of '93 and spent a week without electricity. But the six of us were warm and snug with our wood stove for heat, camp stove for cooking and gravity water. Fortunately, I had just washed all of Canyon's diapers —

cloth — before the power left us.

Growing up in our own rustic abode on the side of a mountain was an education in itself. Before our children could walk, they learned the feel of cool mountain water on their skin as they scooted underwater in our pond between Mom and Dad for a few seconds of suspended breathing. Hiking to the top of the mountain in springtime became an adventure through trillium, pink lady slipper, snake plantain, hearts-a-burstin', and a hundred other happy plants and trees. The kids spent many a day building rock dams in our creek, learning the behavior of the water flowing down the mountain.

Adventure at home, as the Woodward kids build snow caves during the Blizzard of '93.

And as each of our children grew into the awareness that many forms of life other than humans inhabit our natural world, a certain respect and relationship with them was developed. Autumn seemed to have an attraction for spiders, large and small, and could often be seen carrying a cup into which she had herded one so that she could deposit it safely outside our home.

At first wide-eyed and later quite at ease, all of the kids found that contact with a flying, stinging insect rarely results in a sting unless that insect feels that it's about to be confined or that its nest is threatened. Many a wasp that had appeared indoors was allowed to crawl onto an open hand, where it was calmly and safely transported out the nearest door.

At home in our mountain creek — Forest and Rivers pause in their dam building as Autumn pursues a crawdad.

Exploring our creek was fun and often a basic learning experience as rocks were turned over to see who might be living underneath. There were various larvae attached to the rock surfaces, of course, giving high marks to the quality of the water flowing by. But more interesting to the young explorers were the crawdads and salamanders — learning how to keep from harming them as they were caught, and how to grip the crawfish in the proper spot to avoid a pinch from her claws.

There were also snakes in this hands-on classroom. Early on, each of the children learned to recognize the markings of black, garter, king and milk snakes as opposed to the diamond-shaped heads and vertical eye pupils of the copperhead and rattlesnake. All were treated with respect, and those few that presented a hazard were removed to a new and wilder locality.

Our pond, home to tadpoles, frogs and crawdads, also harbors the common water snake, easily confused with the copperhead, until its habits and head are more closely observed. This is our picnic and swimming area, and we are all comfortable cohabiting with the water snakes, particularly since they make themselves scarce while we are in the water. Not all of our guests are of the same mind, however, so we paid Canyon, when he was a little older, two dollars a snake to catch them. We would then give them a temporary bucket home, transport them to the nearby Little Tennessee River and release them.

Two vehicles that we found necessary for mountain life: the "Copper Whopper," a '67 Dodge Crew-cab pickup, and a 1950 (later replaced by a '55) Ferguson tractor.

But sometimes we got distracted. Canyon had caught a water snake and put it in a tub with a little water and a lid for its trip to the river. Later we headed to town for errands at the post office, bank and of course, soccer practice. As I pulled into the bank drive-in, I realized that we'd forgotten to stop at the river and still had the snake with us. A funny, twisted thought flashed through my mind. "What do you think they'd do if we put the snake in the bank's canister and sent it up the vacuum tube?" I asked Canyon.

"Do it! Do it!" he yelled.

"No, no — I'm afraid their sense of humor might not be the same as ours, Canyon," I replied. "In fact it's likely we would get arrested for causing the teller to have a heart attack or at the least to wet her pants, and we certainly wouldn't be welcome at this bank anymore."

And the snake breathed a sigh of relief! At such times, discretion is the lesson to be learned.

~ ~ ~

The pond was our center of activity for family and friends. Swim parties and potlucks always drew a crowd. Basic canoeing and kayaking strokes, as well as wet exits, were learned there. Two picnic tables were built, a cider press purchased from a neighbor and a fall pressing of organic (old and gnarly) apples became a regular and anticipated event.

The kids' forts — made from natural cuttings and scrap building materials — dotted the mountainside not far from the house. Autumn and Rivers used the old string and tin can communications system to stay in touch between their structures.

Forest's fort was a hundred feet higher on the mountain, intended, we thought, as a lookout to warn the others of danger. We only discovered its true purpose sometime later when a well-aimed rolling boulder crashed through Rivers' fort. He and his friend Daniel survived, but had visions of a certain higher fort going up in flame and smoke!

~ ~ ~

A tradition started somewhere in the early years of Autumn, Forest and Rivers, continuing on after Canyon was born. The idea was hatched by the kids without Trish or me being aware of the master plan. On a routine grocery shopping trip, Autumn might say, "Dad, Mom, we need twenty or thirty dollars to pick up some food — it will make you happy," with an air of mystery.

We knew that all of our kids had an interest in cooking, at home as well as on camping trips, acquiring more culinary skills as they grew older. But we were astounded at the creative ability that emerged, particularly from that first conspiracy. In late afternoon, they would shoo us out of the house. "Go take a hike on the mountain, or a swim in the pond — come back at six."

As we approached our front door, it suddenly would swing open, a smiling young maitre-de in coat & tie welcoming us in. (Where on earth did he find such an outfit? In our box of dress-up play clothes?) We were quickly seated at a beautifully appointed table, graced by a fresh bouquet of flowers and handed a menu by the waiter/waitress. Painstakingly hand-lettered, the bill-of-fare presented the mouth-watering, four-course vegetarian dinner we were about to enjoy.

After that first exquisite surprise, Trish and I would be pampered in a similar manner, once or twice a year, the event becoming known as Thunder Creek Café.

~ ~ ~

With our family and home complete, our mountain abode became the place to cook, eat and relax. And, time becoming more flexible, we were more easily able to balance the necessary demands of our lives with the choices we might make in education and adventure.

Did we feel the need to pull back and curtail our outdoor adventures until the kids were "old enough?" Not at all. With at least two and a half years of age between each of the kids, only the youngest required the special attention of being carried on a parent's bike or in a child pack, while the older siblings learned to handle a canoe paddle, hike a trail with a backpack, or take their place on a tandem bike until ready for their own wheels.

Journeys that Intersect

I gaze at Trish as we reach the crest of one more hill, sea lions frolicking in the surf far below us, and think how fortunate I am to have a partner willing to plan and carry out extraordinary family adventures. The off-shore breeze is a welcome caress on our sweat-soaked bodies.

July of 1990 has nearly run its course and our family is biking south on the stunningly beautiful Oregon Coast, sea stacks, shifting mist and long climbs making it a journey to remember. Trish crushes the hills with a full load of camping gear, Autumn (6) snuggled into the seat behind her. I tote a similar set of loaded panniers, with Forest (4) on my bike and Rivers (1) in the child-trailer.

The Severin and Woodward family, bike-camping on the Oregon Coast, July 1990.

"Dad! Dad! Out past the sea lions! There's a whale!"

Forest's young eyes haven't missed a thing — he's just spotted a distant gray whale spouting, nearly a mile out to sea.

Our ten-day route takes us west across northern Oregon, down the coast to the Smith River, across the mountains into the Willamette watershed, through Eugene where our children's bike-trailer was made, and finally north along the Willamette to our starting point at Monmouth. But today we're enjoying the coast, where this biker-friendly state has placed campsites at convenient intervals, campsites that are restricted to those traveling by bicycle or on foot.

It's midafternoon as Trish and I decide to make camp, give the kids play time free of the bike seat confinement and examine our planned route as we are about to turn away from the coast. We pull into the woodsy hiker/biker site of Honeyman State Park and begin to unload the bikes.

"Look!" Autumn is pointing to a picnic table fifty feet away. What appears to be a body on the table top is completely covered by a tattered olive drab army blanket.

"What is it? Who is it? Is it alive or dead?" we wonder. Forest tiptoes to the edge of the table, then returns to our site.

"I saw the blanket move up and down a little," whispers Forest, who appears to have been holding his own breath. "So he must be still alive."

We set up camp as quietly as we can, and speak to each other in hushed tones. An hour later, the body struggles into an upright position, the blanket sliding to the ground, and a grizzled face stares blankly in our direction.

Sending him a few smiles, we furtively glance his way, trying not to prejudge him on appearance. His clothing shows dark stains and considerable wear, his shoes approaching the end of their life. His hair — what there is of it — is matted in disarray and a couple of weeks worth of stubble covers a deeply lined countenance. It appears that all of his possessions are contained in two black plastic bags.

It takes only a moment for Trish and me to express the same thought. "Forest, find out his name and tell him we have plenty if he'd like to eat with us tonight."

Four-year-old Forest is there in a flash, but is in no hurry to return. He climbs onto the table to sit beside his new friend, whose name, he discovers, is Art. To our wonder, they carry on a serious conversation for the next hour and a half.

Two other biking couples arrive to make camp, chat briefly with us about their travels and ours, but completely ignore Art. The weather has been unseasonably cool, so we build a fire at dinner-time. Forest and Art stroll over to our table, Art with a noticeable limp. Trish has put together a pot of pasta with all the veggies we can dig out of our panniers to sauté. Making sure Art has the largest plate, we eat it all, then listen to his story.

Art is 59. He is from Baltimore, having worked all his life, most of it for a construction firm, which laid him off two years ago. His unemployment benefits having ended, he is too young to receive the Social Security he has accumulated and too old to be considered for the job market. He has wandered from one area of the country to another in a fruitless search for work.

One of his black bags is used to collect aluminum cans, one of the few ways he can produce a bit of cash on his own. The police in Reedsport, not friendly to the homeless, told him to move on yesterday. He walked through the night, exhausted, to reach this campground.

Following dinner, and having asked our permission, Art moves his blanket to our table in order to sleep near the campfire. In the morning, we share our cereal with him, make him peanut butter and jelly sandwiches, and slip him a $20 bill. He is grateful and we feel that we've done all that we're able to do. We pack and pedal on, knowing that we will resupply our own food in Reedsport.

But the next evening, as we're camped by the Smith River, Forest startles my complacency with two questions.

"Dad, what will happen to Art? He said he won't go back to Reedsport again."

"I don't know, Forest. I guess he'll keep heading north."

"Did you give him our address and phone number at home?"

"No. I didn't."

We're both silent as I find myself unable to tell my young son that I drew a line, excusing myself from any further responsibility toward Art. As we sit together, I'm not able to justify this to myself, let alone to Forest.

Forest has learned a great deal from his time with Art. But I'm not happy with what he has just learned from me.

~ ~ ~

Years later, another incident caused me to recall Forest's time spent with Art in that campsite on the Oregon Coast. We're halfway through a 200-mile bike/camping journey on Pennsylvania's Great Allegheny Passage. As we pass through a town park, the trail suddenly climbs and I try to downshift too quickly, popping my chain off of its sprocket.

A boy of eight or ten rushes over to ask what happened and, as I tell him, he says that his bike has done the same thing. He is wide-eyed, though, at the heavy panniers and load of camping gear bungeed behind my seat.

"How far are you going?" he asks, perhaps wondering what the chances of his doing a similar journey someday might be. Before I can answer, a man's voice booms from the family picnic table.

"Jimmy, we've told you never to talk to strangers! Get back here right now!"

As I ride down the trail, my thoughts drift back to Forest and Art, their long conversation, the richness of the experience for a four-year-old, and the understanding that came out of that exchange.

What About Schooling?

Autumn draws in a breath, as if about to speak, then quickly gives me that "don't make a sound" look. Afternoon sunlight filters through a thin veil of dancing locust leaves, catching ripples on our pond, threatening to hypnotize the eye that lingers too long. The faintest breeze carries the steady sound of water splashing over the stones at the base of Hazel Falls. Two hawks, nesting somewhere far above us, dip and keen in a mid-air mating dance. The mountain is at peace.

My thirteen-year-old daughter and I are floating on the chilly water of our mountain pond, without sound or movement. With a tilt of her head, Autumn's eyes move from me to a point on the pond's perimeter and back again. Then I see it. The common water snake, perhaps in its third season, is coiled lazily on the pond's overflow pipe. We swim with them regularly.

But, again without a sound, Autumn slowly moves a hand and taps the top of her head. I look once more and can't believe what I am seeing. There, on top of the snake's head, crouches a tiny frog. Do the two of them have a symbiotic relationship, or are they, appetites satisfied, just captured by the magic of this early summer afternoon? It doesn't matter. Our hearts simply smile.

The keen eyes of my daughter have once again pierced the camouflage of the natural world, observing an interaction that I had missed entirely. Is her perception unusual? Perhaps. But I think it's far more likely that she is tuned into the hum of nature around her as a result of growing up with the opportunity to explore and observe.

And is it simply chance that this early learning is occurring amid a natural laboratory that has captured her imagination and enthusiasm? That she is free to hike in any season, cataloging in her mind or journal the changes she finds as plants emerge and bloom, creeks flood, frogs mate and so much more? No, it was intent, not chance, that gave her the opportunity to be different.

~ ~ ~

During Autumn's preschool years, we wrestled often with the question of what her schooling should look like when she reached the mandatory age for entering. Trish, having been a teacher in Atlanta, both in private and inner-city public schools, knew the strengths and shortcomings of each and had a passion for alternative education. And we also knew that by plugging into the public school system, or into a private school — which we couldn't come close to affording — we would immediately eliminate the flexibility that we enjoyed in choosing our own experiences for the education of our children.

In our minds, we were trying to balance giving up our own woodsy classroom and its myriad of possibilities, with the advantage of having access to more traditional, but quality, education. We were aware of homeschooling as a choice, but it was in the back of our minds, and not yet a factor in what would be our ultimate decision on schooling.

By this time our second child, Forest, had arrived, and we found that we could adapt our outdoor and travel activities to accommodate a family of four with a little ingenuity. But now we could see the writing on the wall. The unlimited horizons that Trish and I had acquired in simplifying our lives and freeing our time, the ability to take off on a rewarding family adventure at the most appropriate time, would all come to a screeching halt when Autumn entered school.

There appeared to be only one direction that could solve this dilemma and keep us from losing our family flexibility —

homeschooling. We knew, particularly with Trish's teaching experience and enthusiasm, that this was something we could do. But how rich an experience would this be for the kids? We didn't know very much about it yet.

Would homeschooling be overwhelming for the parents? Would it tie us down in other ways, just as public or private school would have done? How friendly was North Carolina toward homeschooling families? Were there support groups available?

We hadn't waited for a deciding moment to find out. From the time Forest was born, we had been researching the writings of John Holt, *Home Education Magazine*, *Growing Without Schooling*, and North Carolina Statutes. Resources were limited, but what we found was encouraging.

North Carolina, specifically the Department of Non-Public Education under which homeschooling falls, requires only that a notice of intent to operate a home school be filed with DNPE, attendance records be maintained, immunization records be kept (or an exemption filed), and that each student be required to take a nationally standardized test each year. No curriculum is specified, nor is there a requirement to submit any verification of what is being taught, making North Carolina a relatively friendly homeschooling state.

We grabbed it and ran with it. But one thing we knew — we weren't going to make our homeschooling look like traditional schooling, sitting our children down at a desk every day from 8am to 3pm. Sure, there would be plenty of resources available. Trish would appear with bags of books from the local library. Our shelves contained a wide choice of art materials, allowing the kids to choose many directions. Creativity was encouraged, never criticized, for this was the prime reason that our family had chosen to homeschool. Experiential — hands-on — education would be our guiding philosophy.

When we traveled, that travel experience alone would become

the children's education — and ours — for the duration of the trip. Just as this book is a journey that crosses and re-crosses itself in many chapters, so our family's homeschooling — much too narrow a term for these far-reaching experiences — is quite integrated, rather than being divided into sterile subjects.

~ ~ ~

After Trish and I met in the spring of 1979, our lives continued, as they had individually, to be full of real, rather than armchair, activity — backpacking, bicycling, paddling rivers. Watching television did not — and, 38 years later, still does not — exist in our daily routine. We felt, and still feel, that it would be an unnecessary distraction.

So, when we decided to follow the same trail together and move to the mountains, no TV came with us. Our lives were much too full of chores and adventures to be hypnotized by the screen. As a result, this was the life that our children were born into, what they would regard as normal.

"But … when it gets dark in the evening and you're inside, what do you do?" folks would ask. Well, we do what we've always enjoyed — read books. And when the kids began arriving? More books! There were those children's books that appeal to the curiosity of kids — the illustrations, the rhymes, stories with morals or adventures that bear repeating.

But it was not long before these simplistic stories began to give way to chapter books, often in trilogies or longer series — J.R.R. Tolkien, Mary Stewart, Marion Zimmer Bradley, C.S. Lewis, and so many more. Trish would comb the local library for biographies and accounts of social justice heroines and activists, from 150 years ago to the present day. The kids were drawn into the drama of these lives.

Living in the North Carolina mountains, evening quickly became a family time of reading aloud around the warmth of the woodstove, a time of intense anticipation and interest that would not be missed under any circumstances.

Discovering the unknown worlds and adventures that waited within pages could not help but spark a desire for each child to read on her or his own, but also to create stories from their own imagination. Even as a toddler, each child was encouraged to dictate stories in which he or she was the complete master of content and direction — and some of these were wild indeed!

When Canyon was twelve years old, he printed out and made covers for the stories he had written as a homeschooler. There were nineteen booklets in all, his Christmas gift to the family. One of his stories, Tahlequah Secrets, the tale of the events that had been seen by a 300-year-old giant oak tree near our home, won the grand prize in the town of Franklin's 150th anniversary.

While the kids were still too young to write, but overflowing with imagination, Trish would be the master note-taker, and I would later type the story into more permanent form. All of the kids were proud of their creations and would put them together as booklets of stories from time to time, often adding illustrations to liven them up even more.

Soon each child was writing by hand or pecking away at a keyboard as imagination flowed into words. We never corrected spelling, but let phonetic spelling stand on its own, so as not to throw any element of discouragement into the process. This was done with a bit of trepidation on our part, but, as we soon found out, the more reading that each child did, the fewer misspelled words, along with an extensive vocabulary, appeared in her or his own writing, until, indeed, each became an excellent wordsmith without ever having taken a spelling or vocabulary test.

And did this philosophy continue into the teen years? You bet! Outdoor adventures, notes and sketches kept, and friendships made in Central and South America, provided a rich background of material for the creation of stories and poems, as well as painting, drawing and photography. We encouraged these activities simply for the love of it, never requiring a letter grade in any subject. In fact, it is misleading to refer to subjects, since our philosophy of education was largely integrative and experiential.

An important educational activity, both in wild places and among the friendships and traditions of a new country, is that of keeping a journal. Whether reflecting the kindness of new friends, a shift in perspective, or an unexpected act from the heart, the vividness of on-the-spot feelings and events that have been recorded will prove invaluable in the years to come. Those words, drawings and photos form a wellspring of experiences that can provide the basis for a future article or book, a gateway to college, or even a vocation, not to mention being the starting point for a book of this type.

~ ~ ~

Let's open a door to the past and take a look at what our kids were doing with some of their "homeschooling" time. No single day was typical. Creativity was recognized and applauded — never "corrected." Art in its many forms was always a presence, considered just as important as math or science. And free play took no back seat to reading — they were equally important.

The day is stormy; snow has been falling since midnight, the wind piling it up against our windows and front door. Forest has slipped through the partly shielded back door to bring in an armload of red oak. He feeds pieces to the hungry woodstove, lengths that he and his siblings helped split, load and stack before winter marched in.

Canyon is stretched out on the living room rug, surrounded by scotch tape and varying colors of paper, some in strips, other pieces partially folded, some awaiting tiny inscriptions or intricate assembly into awesome creations. He may spend hours on a single project, making you wonder how he conceived and brought it into being.

Rivers is curled up in a comfy chair reading Roald Dahl's *The Twits* and it's not until later, when he invites us to his "Rivers Shivers" theater — for 25 cents admission — that we find he's transformed the book into a play. He has co-opted younger brother Canyon into an accomplice and together they act out a hilarious production, inserting sometimes embarrassing vignettes of Mom and Dad into the script at appropriate moments.

Forest has hidden himself in a corner, where he's shielded his work from curious eyes. He's painting tiny figures — belt buckles, buttons, boots, caps, even faces on characters barely an inch tall — the whole works in fine detail — as a Christmas gift to Canyon. A little later, he switches to wood carving, where the detail is almost as demanding as the painting he's just finished. I still have one of his beautifully sanded and polished miniature kayaks, with paddle, hanging over my window.

Autumn finishes writing one more chapter of her continuing story, *The Secret of the Dark Wood*, and pulls out her fiddle. Having become bored with the Suzuki method in earlier years, she plays us a few Irish tunes, courtesy of her elderly fiddling partner, Lois Duncan, whose friendship has led to a mentoring relationship over the past several years.

Turn the clock slightly forward or backward, as you choose. The day is mild, the creeks on our mountain are running full, and no homeschooler wants to be indoors.

"Can we hike up the mountain, Mom, Dad?"

"Sure, but give us an idea of where you'll be and when you might be back." It takes a little less than an hour to hike to our ridge by an old logging road, through a forest of poplar, hickory, oak, beech and locust.

"Well, we're only going to the upper cove, and not by the road and trail. We want to explore! We'll try to be back by five."

"OK. But stay together and make that try a good one — we don't want to come looking for you." They pack a lunch, an extra shirt for each, and grab a few other hiking essentials. I'm surprised by the route they choose — crossing our lower creek and heading up one of the steeper slopes through dense growths of dog hobble, laurel, and rhododendron — a "laurel hell" in Appalachian mountain parlance.

I stand on our porch and watch them eagerly hop across the creek, then disappear from view as the forest closes behind them. "Did they take water with them?" Trish asks. "They took one liter-size hiking bottle," I reply, but we both know that the kids also have the location of half a dozen mountain springs and seeps embedded in the map they carry in their heads.

Several hours fly by as Trish and I take advantage of the time to get a few of our own projects finished. Before we know it, the sound of voices outside captures our attention and the kids rush in to share their afternoon of discovery.

"You know the tiny pond in the upper cove? Well, there were salamanders mating there! We were real quiet and lay down on the bank. In a few minutes they swam out from under the leaves on the bottom where we could watch them." So much for salamander privacy!

The young homeschooling gang: Forest, Rivers, Canyon and Autumn —
accompanied by Wayah, our Alaskan malamute, pause during a hike on our
North Carolina mountain.

"Why are the trees close to our neighbors so much larger than the
others? Do they grow better because they have more sun?"

"Nope," I reply, "it's because they're much older than most of the
trees in the woods. A century ago, according to our neighbor
Furman Arvey, the mountain was all pasture right to the top, but
the farmers didn't cut the 'line trees' when they cleared land, so
they are a living connection to an older time. When you're on the
mountain again, look in the woods for a fence post that might still
be standing and strands of rusty barbed wire on the ground. They
marked the old boundaries between farms."

"Mom, we didn't see any large animals, but found a lot of deer
tracks around the ford on the creek."

"The deer were probably there, but heard you coming!"

"Well, next time I'm going to take a book by myself, sit beside the
Bear Cave Falls and I bet I'll see more critters if I'm quiet."

"Dad, look at the different leaves we collected! We know most of them, but what are these two?"

"That's a chestnut-oak. The leaf looks similar to the now-extinct chestnut, but the lobes are rounded. The other is a hickory with a leaf grouping, but the outer ends of the leaf are wider than the inner ends, unlike locusts and walnuts."

Another day might find Rivers staying closer to home and work-shop, learning how to split locust into rails and build them into a fence, construct a deck, or terrace the rocky portion of mountain behind the house into flower beds.

Canyon had taken a keen interest in working clay into small figures, then into attractive bowls and plates on the wheel, beau-tifully glazed, from which we still eat all our meals today. Over the years, our good friend Doug Hubbs, a skilled potter, offered his expertise to Canyon as a mentor.

Another longtime friend, Steve Midgett, worked with Forest and his own son, Jacob, through the many steps of making a bow from a locust tree, including the splitting, shaping with a draw knife, steaming for alignment, and tillering for flexibility. Then, of course, the boys would test for accuracy on a stump-shooting course. Later, when we lived in Washington state for a time, Mark Courtney did the same for Rivers, including the making of arrows from Western cedar.

A writer of stories and poetry well beyond her years, Autumn was encouraged by my friend Jim Holechek, who wrote regularly for the *Baltimore Sun* and did a detailed critique of her early stories. As mentioned earlier, Lois Duncan, a mountain fiddler more than six decades older than Autumn, shared her love of Appalachian music with the youngster as friend and mentor.

In the very first year of our homeschooling experience, Trish recognized the need for reaching out to other homeschoolers who might need support. The only statewide and local groups available operated within the confines of a rather narrow religious outlook. We envisioned a support group open to all, without regard to a family's reasons for homeschooling.

After tracking down other families who felt a similar need, perhaps thirty parents and children met at a weekend campout at Morrow Mountain in the central part of the state. From this 1989 gathering emerged Families Learning Together (FLT), meeting two or three times a year at a camp with cabins — from the mountains to the coast — with the purpose of exchanging homeschooling information in an informal and cooperative setting.

These gatherings often drew as many as 120 individuals and were a great source of inspiration to new homeschooling families, as well as old-timers. Each family, including kids, would share not only the responsibilities of cooking and cleaning in a camp kitchen through the weekend, but would present a craft or skill that they wished to contribute to the group. There would be storytelling, paper-making, folk-dancing, fun games, as well as swimming and canoeing if the season were right.

Shortly afterward, we brought together families in our home area and formed a local homeschooling group, Edventurous Learning Families (ELF). Fun events that we planned brought us into contact with area musicians, soapstone carvers, Cherokee historians and much more. Connections with mentors were made. Entire families attended and homeschooled children were soon at ease chatting with adults other than their parents, as well as connecting with the babies and toddlers who were present.

Painting and drawing, skills that both Trish and myself did not possess beyond a very basic level, were enjoyed by all the kids with various mentors through their growing years. Autumn and Rivers carried their painting talents into adulthood, while Forest and Canyon did the same with photography and pottery.

Trish and I, of course, were able to share our own skills with the children, particularly those relating to outdoor adventure, use of tools, cooking (often inventive), gardening, building, and repair of mechanical devices. But even more important were the family discussions of the plight of those less fortunate than ourselves and how changes to our own lifestyle could have an impact on these lives.

Perhaps just as important as being facilitators for our kids' learning paths was the concept of modeling through our own actions the values that we wanted them to learn. Modeling, we found, is always a subtle lesson in learning, whether it be simply observing your parents reading books they love, or as silent observers to a heated public hearing where those same parents are presenting their case for keeping intact a unique and beautiful stretch of country road.

Activism, organizing and networking were tools which the kids came to see in action as Trish would often be the one to identify an issue that demanded attention and then she and I would do the work needed to address it. There have been, and continue to be, environmental and historical issues in which we as a family are deeply involved, including the siting of the Macon County landfill, the detrimental effects of fracking, the replacement of McCoy Bridge, the expansion of NC Hwy 28, and the proposed destruction of Needmore Road.

The kids believed strongly in the organizations that we started, including the statewide and local homeschooling groups mentioned earlier, as well as Voices for Peace, which called for peaceful solutions to conflict, instead of the war with Iraq which our government was advocating. Our children were active participants — of their own choice — in all of these groups.

Modeling went on in other ways as Trish delivered "meals-on-wheels" to county residents who were house-bound, visited with elderly folks in our two local nursing homes, organized a visiting artists' program, and mentored Hispanic students in English skills and future educational possibilities. I wrote homeschooling articles for *Mother Tongue* and *Katuah*, taught black & white photography in the field and darkroom and, as a family, we hosted visitors from other countries through Servas (see page 5).

~ ~ ~

All this is to say that our homeschooling was not a withdrawal from society, but a reaching out for firsthand experience among folks whose lives are different from our own, friends and neighbors whose lives are similar to ours, and the natural environment that makes all life on earth possible. Trish and I could only give so much — it takes mentors from all walks of life to produce an education.

Trish, in her years of teaching in Atlanta, was always more innovative than the curriculum of the school at which she taught, even when the school was considered "alternative." She would take her students outdoors regularly to observe, listen and then draw or write. Inside, they would move furniture, bring in carpet pieces, hang curtains and create "caves" — their own "learning spaces." Play time was a high priority — stimulation for both body and mind — often producing ideas and realizations that the kids brought back to share with teacher and classmates. All of these teaching innovations transferred well to the style of learning that we wanted our children to experience.

Trish and I have felt for years, perhaps reaching back to our own school days, that concentration on tests and grades gets squarely in the way of creativity and the joy of discovery that a child should be experiencing. As a result, our children never saw a grade until they graduated from our homeschool and we had to produce a transcript, the exception being grades for courses they might take concurrently at our local high school or community college. Similarly, they never took a test until required by North Carolina law to do so. We wanted each of them to have a love of learning for its own sake, for what captured their imagination, rather than performing to meet some arbitrary standard.

For these same reasons, we felt that assigned homework —

especially in a child's early years — was an unnecessary distraction from a genuine interest in exploratory learning. That homework gobbles up the little bit of unstructured time a child might have for rich and rewarding family interactions.

~ ~ ~

Trish so ably summed up what we wanted our children to take with them when they left their time of adventuring with us:

- Confidence and honesty, with compassionate, loving hearts.

- Questioning minds, without boundaries, ever changing and expanding.

- A love for learning and all that life has to offer.

- A creative spirit as a way of life.

- A responsibility to engage with the suffering of the world's people.

- A sense of adventure and a strong relationship with nature and wild country.

- The responsibility for defending the natural environment in which we live.

- The courage to take risks in life and to walk on the edge.

Ah, but what about college requirements for homeschoolers, you ask — SAT, ACT and grade transcripts? First of all, we made it clear to our children that a college education was not a prerequisite to a complete, or "good" life. It was simply a choice, and in our family's case, one that could only be made with financial assistance, whether by scholarship or loan. In the end, however, they all chose the college route, each with a well-earned and welcome scholarship, and of course we did all we could to support the choice once each had made that decision.

Since the children had all graduated "high school" as homeschoolers, to a large extent with self-directed learning, what did they present in their applications to satisfy college entrance requirements.

A *transcript*, of course — which meant that we, as parents, would dissect their tapestry of experience, divide it into appropriate subjects, and assign a letter grade.

An *ACT test score*, and *SAT subject tests*, as might be required by the particular college to which they were applying. They were familiar with taking these tests — required by NC law — and, as is typical of homeschoolers in general, their results were significantly above the average of public school students.

An *individual portfolio*, highlighting unusual life experiences, individual creativity and leadership, and a commitment to social justice, as well as the more ordinary aspects of education, was the key to getting the admissions counselor to take a second look. These portfolios contained extensive student commentary, supporting photographs, and were often fifty pages in length.

With so many college applicants from public or private high schools having straight "A"s and leadership positions in sports or clubs, it falls on the homeschooler to present the "unusual" in order to stand out and be considered for scholarships as well as admission. Creativity will have served the homeschooled student well if she can show in her portfolio, her published art or stories, service projects where she has been the planner and coordinator, and other endeavors demonstrating individual initiative.

There were a few schools who simply said, "If we didn't ask for it, we won't look at it," when it came to a portfolio. They didn't, and missed some promising prospects by taking that attitude. On the other hand, of those who did take a look, offers of acceptance were made by Brown, Duke, Guilford, Harvard, UNC-Chapel Hill and Yale among others.

In keeping with our family philosophy of integrated learning, there was a mix of educational experiences among our children.

Under a policy of the county school board, a homeschooling child who took two courses at the local high school could participate in extra-curricular activities at that school.[2] As a result, the kids became leaders in school service groups and projects, and excelled in sports such as cross-country, soccer, and tennis.

As proof of their ability to handle college-level courses, they also studied subjects at Western Carolina University and Southwestern Community College as homeschoolers. In fact, Rivers had completed an associate's degree at the latter school by the time he finished his "high school" years, giving him advanced standing when starting his studies at UNC-Chapel Hill.

In retrospect, with all four children having finished their college undergraduate years, we can look back on the twisting path that our children's education took, following the faint trail on a map, peering into dark caves, running wild rivers, climbing glacier-clad mountains, and gathering wisdom from those who live a simpler life than we do, and simply say … it worked.

[2] North Carolina is not uniform from school district to school district in its policy of accommodating homeschoolers in public school activities, and some states prohibit it entirely. Always check with your local public school district — no matter which state you reside in — if your child is interested in extra-curricular participation at a particular school.

Riding a Westward Wind
June and July, 1996

Several times in the growing years of our family, we followed the urge to explore the trails, rivers and back roads of the West, introducing our children to special places that were familiar to Trish and myself, and adding a host of others that were new to all of us. The summer of '96 was one of those times. Autumn was 12, Forest 10, Rivers 7 and Canyon 3.

Departing home in the summer would mean missing cool swims in our pond, leaving an abundant crop of blueberries and blackberries and, most of all, the organic garden harvest which would be entrusted to other hands. A friend who needed a temporary home would housesit and share a bit of love with our cats and Alaskan malamute.

We pictured adventure around each bend, planned for surprises as best we could, and turned our faces to the road.

~ ~ ~

"Are you going to swoop us?" asked Canyon, who, at three, was already becoming used to the way our family handled road trips.

"You bet!" Mom replied, "Middle of the night."

We had found that the "swooping" technique worked quite well for us. All would be prepared the night before — our van completely loaded, kids' sleeping spots designated, and navigation aids within reach of the driver. The kids would tuck into bed dressed for travel. When our alarm went off in the wee hours, Trish and I would quickly dress and carry or guide each of the children to the van. Into the night we'd go, rolling toward a new adventure.

Within minutes, sleep would return to the kids and perhaps half an hour later to the off-duty driver. A silent start over dark and lonely roads soon spun out the miles behind us. Around eight o'clock, squirming in the rear might start and then, "I'm hungry, Dad. Are we going to stop?"

Soon the whole crew would be awake, looking for a convenient place to grab egg biscuits and take a bathroom break. The stop would be relatively short as we tried to keep to a planned schedule to avoid large city rush-hours as we passed by. No matter the time of day or night, the Gateway Arch in St. Louis was not to be missed, nor the first sighting of the Front Range of the Rockies.

~ ~ ~

Poudre River Canyon, north and west of Fort Collins, CO and one of our favorite areas, is our initial destination on this trip. A small campsite offers privacy for our tent, well-removed from RVs and trailers. We relax and restore our energy, in preparation for enjoying the canyon and celebrating Trish's June 7 birthday.

With our professional rowing rig, we're prepared to raft, but with our first look at the high water roaring down the canyon, we scratch that as a family option. There are plenty of inviting trails to hike, however, and the bicycling is demanding but beautiful in the upper reaches of the Poudre. We enjoy both.

Near the top of the canyon, we hike six miles (roundtrip) along the Big South Fork, which is thundering down its gorge just like the Poudre, with intimidating rapids. The hike is beautiful, through aspen, along old rock slides, and over footbridges above boisterous creeks running high from snow melt.

Canyon does a super job of hiking for a three-year-old — he would have done the whole thing — except that we are chased by a thunderstorm the last mile and a half, so he rides out on my shoulders for speed.

We've waited until our second camp is set up at Aspen Glen to celebrate Trish's birthday. The kids have picked fresh flowers, including a lilac, which smile at her from one of our water bottles on the picnic table.

Canyon has made Trish a picture book, Rivers a hand-carved soapstone owl, Forest a necklace and miniature woven hanging, and Autumn a wooden doll with hand-sewn clothing. I give her a composite photo of all four kids and a card good for a day to herself and an hour backrub. Our gifts are kept compact for traveling, but even at home, they are personal and homemade.

The next morning, I bike up the canyon to Chambers Lake and then down the Laramie River Road. The early hours are refreshing with views of snow-capped peaks, stream-filled meadows, bounding deer, and even a moose on the far side of a string of beaver ponds.

When Trish and the kids overtake me in the van, we switch drivers and she and the older kids bike the remaining miles to Woods Landing, just over the Colorado/Wyoming border. A young couple has recently bought the store and cabins, and we all discuss running the Laramie River, but again the high water discourages us.

So, instead, we head north to the town of Laramie, then east about 20 miles to Vedauwoo to camp. The Vedauwoo rocks are just as unusual as I remembered from camping there almost forty years ago, and the kids have a great time climbing on them and playing soccer with other campers.

We enjoy an early breakfast, followed by a four-mile-loop hike around Turtle Rock. The trail is lovely in the morning light, passing many beaver ponds, one with a very large lodge. We spend a second night at Vedauwoo, and at dusk, three separate storms bring spectacular lightning and an hour of rain.

The drive over the Snowy Range is breathtaking — so early in the season that the lakes are completely frozen over and there is practically no traffic through the snow-capped mountains. It's a very inviting area — Poudre Canyon, Laramie River Road to Wood's Landing, Laramie, Snowy Range, Saratoga — for a bicycle camping adventure. (And that was just the trip we did a year later in 1997.)

After a steep descent from the Snowy Range, we enjoy some homemade ice cream at Saratoga and enquire about rafting the North Platte and Encampment rivers. They're running high, of course. An outfitter gives us information and will run shuttle, but Trish likes the looks of the river even less than the Laramie, so we move on.

Wyoming 70 is a wild and lonely highway that we follow over the Continental Divide, leaving it at one point to check out a dirt road that descends to Battle Creek. With a forest of fir and huge aspens that beckons to us, we decide to keep exploring the dirt road — a big mistake!

With the record winter snowfall, water is running down the road as if it were a creek. After negotiating mud-hole after mud-hole, we become mired in one so deep that the van's tailpipe is bubbling away under water. Following two hours of innovative extraction, we are on the loose once more — in the forward direction.

In all that time, we have seen no other vehicle, but a posse of mounted cowgirls materializes to tell us that we're approaching private property and must turn back. We try to explain how disastrous that direction would be for the van. They shrug and watch us continue on.

After carefully opening and closing a number of cattle gates and apologizing to various ranch occupants, we at last emerge onto a public gravel road in the valley of the Little Snake River. Water is bursting over the banks and we watch Sandhill cranes feeding in the meadows.

It's on to Lander, through Rawlins and past Split Rock, one of the major landmarks of the Oregon Trail. As we approach Lander, the sky ahead is black and snake lightning gives us quite a show. We hit the downpour in town, but as we turn up the Sinks Canyon by the Popo Agie River to make camp, the storm is left behind and the kids are delighted to be able to play with other campers their own age.

Reaching the high northwestern shoulder of the Wind River Range, the breathtaking sight of the Tetons beyond stops us in our tracks as it always does. Rugged peaks rising impossibly from the valley below, storm clouds swirling through the gaps, alternately hiding and revealing stark rocky faces. The country through which Trish and I had backpacked on our wedding trip fifteen years earlier. We all pause to absorb the sight.

Entering Grand Teton National Park at the Moose Gate and, finding Jenny Lake Campground full, we drive on to Signal Point. Lunch finished amid the busyness of crowds, Delta and United flights from Jackson Hole taking off over our heads, we realize that this is not why we've come west and turn toward National Forest.

The road changes to gravel and we carefully ford a rushing creek, remembering well that the van is not an ATV. Unusual red hills appear before us and in another five miles we're at two Forest Service sites. We make camp at Crystal, beside the swollen Gros Ventre River, a lone heron fishing near the opposite shore.

With the lack of playmates, our kids are not as enthused about camping here as Trish and I are. However, within minutes of finishing their camp chores — preparing tent, sleeping and cooking spaces, along with gathering firewood — their creativity takes over. The terrain is ideal for constructing their own "Roxaboxen," a community of stone pathways, hidden homes and more, based on Alice McLerran's delightful children's book of the same name.

The next morning, we park at Warm Spring and all bike a 23-mile loop through the Park, the big peaks of the Tetons dominating the view everywhere. While biking, a red-tailed hawk makes a strike, scrambles a moment in the roadside grass, and takes flight again not six feet from my bike, with a gopher squealing in its talons. If only my camera had been at the ready! Our loop takes us through Kelly and Moose, where we stop for juice and crackers. Near the end, we enjoy a swim in the warm spring, with bullfrogs serenading us.

The early dawn makes it easy to get started toward Yellowstone and we're on the road by 5:15am. Grazing buffalo appear in the countryside and we arrive at Old Faithful three hours later. Trish tucks in for a nap after hanging out our hand-washed laundry in the parking lot, determined to not be part of the "Yellowstone Tourist Trap."

An Old Faithful eruption captures our attention, then the kids and I walk a 3-mile loop through many unusual geysers, hot pools and mud pots. These seldom-seen features inspire the kids and they go wild with photos. We see marmots, too, but by the time we get back, the park is overrun with people. Leaving a beautiful national park to the crowds, we head out along the Gallatin River.

As we wind our way into Montana on secondary roads, we're once again surrounded by lightning, black clouds and heavy rain. The Missouri River is flooding beside us. We find a JB's in Helena, and celebrate Fathers Day with dinner out.

After dinner, I'm honored with Fathers' Day gifts — drawings from Canyon, a clay bead necklace from Rivers, a braided hanging (we hang it on the van mirror) of many colors from Forest, an unusual tiny stone and a card good for back scratch, foot rub, etc. from Autumn, and a beautiful poem from Trish.

Soon we're heading north up the Swan River Valley, needing a place to stay put for a few days. At Swan Lake, Deer Lick Resort catches our eye and we check out the cabins. We settle on what seems to us like a small "palace" for four nights — huge kitchen and two separate bedrooms, one with a king-sized bed. In the living room are two sofa-beds and a fancy old-time woodstove.

With the rain and falling temperature, we crank up the stove immediately. Forest has a great time chopping and splitting firewood into kindling. Settling into our cozy cabin, I make vegetable-tofu soup and cornbread while Trish takes a nap.

We all sleep late in a quiet space again — what a luxury! Happy Birthday, Forest! Trish makes a delicious breakfast of hash browns, scrambled eggs (Autumn cooks those), orange juice and bear claws. Gifts are opened at 10:18am, as Forest officially turns ten.

Canyon has four pictures he's drawn for Forest, Rivers a soapstone wolf head he carved, Autumn a complete book of stories that she's written, Trish a photo of Forest rowing on the Green River, and Dad a hand-made knife sheath.

We rent a fishing rod and Forest has fun fishing off the dock with a new friend, Jeff. The rhubarb pie I bake for Forest's birthday is makeshift — no flour, so pancake mix for crust, brown sugar for sweetness, and a little cornstarch to try to thicken the well-cooked rhubarb and apples. The substitutions work well, and we all quickly devour it.

The ancient woodstove has felt good every night and morning and we learn that we were in the coldest spot in the U.S. (Alaska included) at 31°F yesterday. And we're in the middle of summer about to head out on a bike trip?!

Off in the rain, we stop for breakfast in Kalispell. No bike trip today, with the wet weather. Instead, we head up to Glacier National Park, where we find that Logan Pass has been closed again by snow, after being open for only a day.

Our fingers are crossed for a fair-weather start to our week-long bike trip, though it's still raining as we camp a mile west of Rexford, MT. This will be Rivers' first family bike trip with a full load on his own bicycle. Our planned route will take us across Lake Koocanusa — a name blended from the Kootenai River and the two countries which the lake spans — into wild, relatively uninhabited territory west of the lake until we reach the towns of Libby and Troy.

A mist-filled morning without rain raises our spirits. Starting at 11:30am, we have a seven-mile downhill run to Lake Koocanusa. On the way, a deer bounds out of the shifting mist and across the road, nearly colliding with Rivers, just before we reach the bridge.

And the road goes on forever! Wild and lonely, and so much longer than we had told Rivers!

The bridge is being repaired, has only one lane open, and a sign prohibiting bicycles and pedestrians. Being Sunday, no work is in progress and no one in sight. The bridge is vital to our route. We cross.

Showers return and follow us through the early afternoon — then we have an hour of sunshine. The road on this side of the lake is like a 20-foot-wide paved bike path. We have it all to ourselves — maybe one vehicle an hour.

A truck stops, and the driver says there is a black bear on the road in the direction we're traveling — we keep a sharp eye out, but see nothing. We guess the bear got warned that a bicycle posse was traveling the road in her direction!

The road is scenic, but later in the afternoon the rain sets in again with a steady drizzle. My trip estimate from looking at the map is four miles short of actual, and by the time we've reached the place where our campground should be, we've ridden 42 tough miles. Trish does a great job of encouraging Rivers for the last six of them, but now it's 6:30pm.

Smiles are hard to come by near the end of the first day's biking!

There is only a small clearing where the campground is shown on the map, but at last we find a "make-do" camping spot at the end of a short dirt road. The tents are set up facing each other, with our tarp covering the space between. Food is hung a good distance away, and I find a spring near the lake from which to draw water.

A huge flock of Canada geese heads north up the lake, flying low. The moon shows, and the lake briefly reflects a rosy afterglow.

I think the weather is clearing, but it's not. Rain sets in again, staying with us all night and into morning.

It continues through breakfast and camp pack-up — always a downer. We're rolling by 10am, with a light shower now and then. The air is chilly. We stop at the Libby Dam for a few minutes, then speed downhill to our intersection with Montana Hwy 37. Rivers is tired and sore, and I've felt a little sick during the morning. Autumn offers to carry my tent, bless her!

There is rain in the night, the morning weather looking mixed. We pack wet and head out under a light sprinkle. Montana's Hwy 2 has a good six-foot-wide shoulder. Rivers and I take the lead all the way to the junction for Bull Lake.

Before arriving there, we stop at the Falls of the Kootenai, where *The River Wild* (starring Meryl Streep and Kevin Bacon) was filmed. The river at that spot is quite impressive.

Halfway to Bull Lake, Little Joe Montana's Café beckons us to stop for a quick root beer. At the lake, we're the only campers, and as we set up the tents and tarp, the local air force arrives and we realize why no other humans are here. The mosquitoes are abundant and some of the fiercest we've ever encountered. We had planned to lay over at Bull for a day to enjoy the swimming, but everyone agrees — forget it!!

It rains from 4 to 8am, forcing us to pack up wet and fast again. Rivers, with three bowls of granola, keeps the lead with Trish all the way to Troy. Canyon switches to Dad's bike — the load feels good, like old times, as we average 12.5 mph for the day.

La Vi RV Park turns out to be a delight — reasonable, and very nice folks. We set up in a private corner by the bathhouse, where we can eat and do our laundry.

The light on the high mountains to the east is spectacular — many color variations, with striking golden light on the forests contrasting with dark, dark storm clouds above. It rains all night.

Trish scoots into Troy to do an early shopping, and when she comes back the kids all surprise us with 15th wedding anniversary cards that they've made before we left! And Autumn has crafted a beautiful wooden plaque with burned-in letters, ferns and crystal.

The sun plays hide-and-seek for an hour, lets us get underway for 30 minutes, and then ducks away while storm clouds boil up behind us. The shoulder on U.S. 2 to the west is only a foot wide, miniscule compared to the six-foot width to the east.

The downpour arrives, and we pedal hard to take shelter under the eaves of a nearby store. We wait this one out, but rain follows us all day — no more sun at all.

The climb up along the Kootenai is long and steep — Rivers handles it well. Soon we're at our turn onto the Yaak River Road, the rain still with us. This road has a lot of "up" also, with few places to stop. So few, in fact, that we end up having lunch beside a group of dumpsters, since places to lean our loaded bikes have been so scarce. What a sight we are!

The Yaak Falls campsite is scenic and inviting, even in the rain. The rest of the family sets up the tarp and starts a fire (Forest is an expert at coaxing a flame out of wet wood) while I ride to our friends' place on Seventeen Mile Creek, but Barbara and John aren't home — just their dog and two cats guarding mountain bikes, kayaks and a canoe.

Barbara and John's place is in a beautiful setting, a log home with a log barn. The second floor of the barn looks dry and spacious — a great place to hang out on a rainy night! My note left at the door tells them of our camping spot tonight as well as our plans for the next two nights. I bike back to Yaak Falls, where we set up camp and make dinner.

Rain continues through the night and into the morning. By now, we have our "standard" set-up at every campsite — the tent doors close to each other, and the tarp rigged to cover the gear in the area between tents, like a giant vestibule.

Our Yaak River camp, Canyon tending the fire.

I've just lowered the food bags (from out of "bear reach") when Barbara drives up in an ancient VW bus and invites us to a pancake breakfast at the house. We pack in record time and quickly bike the 4½ miles to their place. The ride up their lane through a sea of lupines almost overwhelms our senses with magical fragrance — like a scene from *The Wizard of Oz*.

The family is all there — Barbara's husband, John, son Ian (18) and daughter Willow (15). The pancakes — cooked on their wood-burning stove — are superb, as is the huckleberry sauce made from their hand-picked berries.

The kids have a great time with Willow, visiting kittens in the barn and bouncing on the trampoline while Trish and I discuss travels, outdoor pursuits, rural living and life philosophies with Barbara and John for 3½ hours. They've traveled many of the same paths that we have — New Zealand, Kauai, Grand Canyon in winter, etc.

Roasting biscuits at the Yaak Camp.

We finally say goodbye — they have to leave tomorrow to perform timber surveying — and bike on to Pete Creek. The weather seems to be turning — enough clouds mixed with sun to keep the day comfortable for riding, but *no rain*!

The moon peeks out for the first time this week, as we snuggle into our Yaak River campground, surrounded by huge boulders.

A sparkly blue day at last! We could lay over a day, but decide to ride on. In three miles, we come to the Yaak Store and add food for the last leg of biking. The ride is beautiful, past mature forest, a few meadows and across the West Fork of the Yaak — some pretty good hills at the end.

Caribou Camp sits right on the creek — a pretty spot with only three sites. One is occupied, but we get the nicest, a walk-in site across a little foot bridge over the creek.

The family has ridden 200 miles and I'll ride a few more tomorrow when I go over the pass to get the van. What a great job the kids have done riding under load, and in such rainy weather!

I'm up early on a chilly morning, riding toward the pass by

5:40am. The temperature at dawn is just above freezing. It's a grunt, but not as tough as I had thought — beautiful views, lots of bounding deer and even a cow moose on the road. By 7:30am, I'm at the top — 11 miles from Caribou camp — cold but soaked with sweat.

Autumn pauses at Yaak Falls, sometimes run by bold kayakers.

I change to a dry shirt and wind shell and begin a rapid descent. Within half an hour I'm at Lake Koocanusa, scooting across the "no bicycles" bridge (did we really plan for the return crossing to be on a Sunday again, with no construction crews present?) and starting the ascent toward Rexford on the opposite side of the lake.

Getting the van and retracing my route, I find another biker walking his bike about a third of the way up. He accepts my offer of a ride to the top, so we load his bike and gear on the van rack. I give him my last cookie as he gets out at the pass. Several hours later, he limps into camp with a broken brake cable and gladly accepts our spare.

Two fellows camped at the top of the hill come down and tell us they've chased a brown bear away from their camp and that it's heading our way. We make sure our food is secure and that there is nothing out that would attract the bear. Suddenly we realize that Canyon is nowhere to be seen.

Mom and Rivers bike along the Yaak River on a rare sunny day.

Five minutes of calling his name produce no results. Our anxiety increases. The five of us search within an imaginary circle extending a couple of hundred yards from our camp. Still no Canyon. Or bear.

Forest descends to the creek and in a matter of moments shouts back toward camp, "Here he is!" As we all dash toward Forest, a small grinning figure emerges from under the bridge.

"Didn't you hear us all calling you, Canyon?" Mom asks with a mixture of anger and relief. "There's a bear coming this way." "I heard you. I just liked being under the bridge — it's cozy there. My fort." The bear apparently knew better than to become part of this scenario and must have veered off into calmer territory.

This was not a first. That spring, in Atlanta's main REI store, Canyon had disappeared, provoking a frantic family search that included every nook and cranny in the store, as well as the parking lot. Again, it was Forest who noticed that a backpack in the wall display had sprouted legs and the three-year-old that they belonged to was behind it, persistently trying to open a bag of gorp pilfered from a nearby trail snack display.

When we find a phone and call our house-sitter at home, the news is not good. Our malamute, Wayah, companion on so many mountain hikes, has died, my son David burying her beneath a special tree at his place. Terrific rains have wreaked havoc on our gravel road. Autumn is in tears about Wayah and Forest cries later at bedtime. We all miss her.

Canyon has been thinking about death, also. He's drawn a very small, intricate picture on his magnetic drawing board. He points to it and says, "When we die, the fire will fire all of this, won't it?"

~ ~ ~

After brief visits with good friends in Missoula, and Trish's uncle Jack in Spokane, we head once again for the backcountry trails, this time on the Olympic Peninsula. We arrive at Sol Duc, pack for a mid-afternoon start, and make camp after covering only 3½ miles. We're all tired, cook a late tortilla dinner and are soon asleep in our tents.

Trish has warned the kids that the next day's climb will be steeper and that an early start is in order. We've found that the cool of the morning air helps our energy last longer, and if we can get to our destination sooner, then there will be time to explore and play.

Yesterday, I twisted my ankle rather severely, but with a cold-water soak and a night's rest, I thought it might heal. Not yet. It's hard to put much weight on it, so Trish and Autumn take about 15 pounds of my load — more than they should.

On the way up, we stop for lunch where the trail crosses the river. The water is numbing, but bright with sunshine, so we all enjoy a dip and I'm able to soak my ankle again. Swimsuits are in order as a courtesy to other hikers who might pass that way as we enjoy plunge after plunge into the icy pool.

Autumn leaps into the icy water!

We reach Sol Duc Park, our camp for the night, ready to relax, with a good part of the afternoon remaining. There is less solitude here as several sites are already occupied, so Trish leaves her pack and goes on to scout for other campsites. When she returns, with a report of an ideal site a half-hour away, she finds that we've already set up camp.

I felt that it was better to rest my injured ankle early and the kids are already having fun creating tiny boats and racing them in the creek. After dinner, we hike to an open area where we watch a herd of perhaps fifty elk grazing on a distant mountain that is still glowing in the late sunlight.

Rather than packing up, hiking and then camping at the High Divide, we decide to spend two nights at Sol Duc Park and day-hike to the top. The weather is exquisite — typical for July in Washington state — a great payback for the rain we've endured while biking.

All of us enjoy the day on the High Divide — one of Trish's favorite outdoor places. We pass close to an incredibly beautiful waterfall and climb to views that are magnificent — many glaciers in sight and mist boiling up from lakes in the deep valleys. Three deer join us for a while and we spot a bald eagle in the top of a tree by one of the lakes, to the delight of the kids.

On the High Divide Trail, Canyon in the lead.

Clouds begin to roll in from the west and, as we hike back to camp, there is no doubt that the weather is changing. A noisy Boy Scout troop that has set up nearby is the determining factor in whether we camp or move on. After grabbing quick naps, we all head down the trail far enough that we can hike out the next day.

At three, Canyon is our inspiration. Having already hiked down from the High Divide, he now adds another four miles to his day's total. "He's a real trooper," as Trish notes in her journal. We choose a pleasant campsite beside a tumbling brook, just inside the "campfire permitted zone."

The brook apparently relocated itself about ten feet west of its present course at some recent point in time, and now the bridge ends right in the center of the rushing torrent. The kids gather wood and start a campfire. Dinner is cooked, devoured, and the remaining food hung on the bear wire. Just as we turn in, the rain begins.

The drizzle persists right through the night and we pack up wet in the morning. The hike out — about five miles — is not difficult and the kids do a terrific job. Canyon is the "red & black checkered engine," often talking to the caboose by telephone. We stop at Sol Duc Falls, an impressive, deep gorge with cataracts shooting sideways.

Three Japanese girls at the falls smile and say, "picture?" I think they want me to take a photo of the three of them and gesture toward their camera. But instead, the one that asked steps up beside me, pulls my sweaty body close, and her friends take photos.

After looking forward to a family soak in the hot springs, the cost discourages us and we ask the kids if we could substitute a night in a cabin instead. They're enthused at the prospect, so we head for the north coast where we find a good deal on one at Sekiu. It's a great place to shower, dry out gear and generally regroup for the next adventure. The fog horn lends a melancholy feeling to the night as ships cautiously churn their way through the Straits of Juan De Fuca.

~ ~ ~

We want to introduce the kids to the Pacific Coast of the Olympic Peninsula and Trish has chosen an easy 3½-mile hike from Ozette to Cape Alava to make that possible. It's a flat hike, partially over boardwalks. Trish and I will carry an extra load so we tell the kids that they can take day packs instead of backpacks, even though we're camping for the night. They're delighted.

The backpack in is easy, though the rain is with us once more. I absentmindedly leave my camera at the trailhead shelter and Autumn sprints back to retrieve it, finding it gone. Eventually, she tries the ranger station, where a kind-hearted camper has turned it in.

The wind never ceases and gusts threaten to carry away our tents as we're setting up camp. But the weather is only a minor nuisance when matched against the majesty of the cape where we're camping. Rocky sea stacks rise out of the ocean and thousands of huge driftwood logs form a beach of their own. The boys and I work for several hours creating a snug driftwood cave of moveable pieces blended with those we can't budge.

Rivers and Forest in the driftwood hideaway at Cape Alava on the Washington Coast.

The cave is a welcome refuge from the wind, and we take advantage of it, reading books and writing in our journals. But the night is far from relaxing. Back in our tents, even though they're staked securely, the wind whips the nylon with a vengeance, making it hard to sleep.

Rain persists, with sporadic showers, pelting us as we pack up camp and hike back to Ozette. But then ... we should be used to it by now!

~ ~ ~

As our Western adventure draws to a close, we feel our North Carolina mountains beckoning once more. It's a long road from Ozette to Franklin, and our route takes us south, through Olympia to Portland, then east along the gorge of the Columbia River. Tugs, barges, dams, trains, and tunnels delight Canyon and the other children.

With a 75-mph speed limit, the miles fly by; we pass our goal of Boise and expect to be in Utah by evening. But this is not to be. We've made just over 600 miles when the left rear tire goes flat — something sharp has made a finger-sized hole in the almost-new mud/snow tire. Worse yet, the spare is completely flat.

The temperature is over 100° F and a state trooper stops to tell us we're about twelve miles from the nearest help. I pump four or five hundred strokes into the spare from the mini bike pump and we limp into Glenn's Ferry, barely off the rim. No one with tires is open, but we get more air from a friendly fellow in a paint shop, who also directs us to the campground.

The campground is neat and attractive, and is located on an historic spot on the Snake River, Three Island Crossing. This was a very difficult river ford on the Oregon Trail, where many pioneers lost wagons, belongings and some even their lives. We enjoy a quiet evening and a striking sunset.

The tire is replaced, and by 9am we're on the road, making good time again. We soon cut the corner of Utah and are heading east into Wyoming. As we approach Laramie, the clouds are a spectacular silver and black with a brilliant rainbow beneath. Lightning flashes through the rainbow from behind — wow! We've never before seen anything like it!

But the transition from outdoor activity to long days in the van is difficult for the kids as they begin picking at each other and getting on our nerves. Behavior in the van is at an all-time low, and a planned stop to eat out at JB's is cancelled, much to the consternation of the kids. Instead, we head for a campground and fix sandwiches for dinner.

Trish and I realize we need to slow down, so we head into Laramie to play in the park, pick up groceries and enjoy ice cream cones. Amazingly, a woman in the park — herself pulling a

Burley trailer — remembers seeing us in New Zealand in 1988 when we were touring with Autumn and Forest in a Burley! She is a native of the Netherlands and met her husband doing a "round-the-world" bike trip while they were in New Zealand.

On returning to camp, we rock-climb again, starting in the Vedauwoo Glen area — all four kids this time — and make it to the top. They all seem to be natural climbers.

Our plan now is to stop early, so we get a motel room in Salina, Kansas, where we relax in the pool and have pizza delivered. The evening is spent watching the Olympics and we are delighted to find several segments of the whitewater events presented. I see many familiar faces on the screen.

Twenty hours later, following an all night drive, we bump slowly up our mountain road. The silence feels odd, and then we realize what's missing — the singsong greeting of Wayah, our beloved malamute and companion of a dozen years.

The van doors fly open and the rush is on to be first in our comfy claw-foot bathtub!

~ ~ ~

Trish sums up our odyssey with her own journal words:

After eight weeks, we arrive back home — a good trip which is hard to have end in many ways. The kids were great travelers most of the time and I think that the intensity of such a long vacation brings us all together more focused. I came home feeling very relaxed with many new thoughts and ideas!

Only three weeks later, I'm doing preliminary planning on a winter trip to Peru! Oh, to be "cursed with the gypsy blood!" But such adventure lies ahead...

Journey of the Heart
Embracing Friendship and Love in Peru

In early 1997, after reading Ethan Hubbard's Journey to Ollantaytambo, seeking the advice of a good friend who was native to Peru, and discussing the possibilities of a learning experience in that country as a family, we decided to take the month of February to venture into territory new to us. Autumn was 13, Forest 10, Rivers 8 and Canyon 4. As we gradually reached beyond the stereotyped views presented by our State Department and well-meaning but poorly informed friends, we became enthused about the adventure. As it turned out, we made lasting friendships, and would return to Peru 17 years later to embrace old friends and see how marriages and births had shaped their families.

~ ~ ~

As our Aero Peru flight descends through the hot, sticky air of February — summer for the Southern Hemisphere — the sprawling coastal city of Lima slowly transforms itself from a dark dot on the map of South America into the living, breathing home to nearly ten million souls.

Our family has confidently brushed aside the fears of well-meaning friends and relatives. "It's no place for the kids." "Don't drink the water." "Be careful what you eat, you'll get sick." "You'll be robbed." "People disappear there." "We won't rest until you're back."

Self-assurance or arrogance? Are we really certain that our family of six is prepared for the unknown into which we are stepping? A glimpse of the scene on the far side of the airport's glass barrier shows the turmoil of those who are desperately trying to gain a bit of pocket change or more from the wealthy tourist. Men and women hawking taxis and hotels. Aggressive luggage carriers. And, most heart-wrenching of all, the ten-year-old girls, cradling tiny babies, asking for donations to buy milk.

Later, we will learn that the babies — at least the majority of them — are rented from their real mothers, the English word "milk" memorized, and the "desperate juvenile mother" may produce as much income on a good day at the airport as a working adult elsewhere. Most taxis and hotels are legitimate, but be careful — don't let luggage out of your sight — and remember, the person guiding you expects a tip from you and a cut of the taxi fare or lodging cost. Sure, the need is often legitimate, but the airport with its arriving tourists is also a prime target for scam artists.

But that night, by planning ahead, we've made our arrival much smoother. Each of us, including Canyon, who has just celebrated his fourth birthday, carries only a day pack for the month ahead. No checked baggage for any of us. We've booked a pair of reasonable rooms before leaving home. And best of all, a smiling face and a "Woodward Family" sign catch our eyes before we're swallowed by the waiting crowd.

Many hostels and hotels will have you met at the airport by someone on their staff. "Staff" may consist of only the proprietor and her spouse, who often go out of their way to make you feel comfortable, as a gesture of friendship and perhaps in hope of a favorable future recommendation. In our case, the smiling face is Pepi, brother-in-law of our good friend at home, Elena, a native of Peru.

We spend two nights at our Lima rooms, taking the day in between to explore the part of the city which surrounds us. We walk the streets, watching people as they watch us. The collectivas roll past in the heavy traffic, the "caller" shouting the destination of his particular vehicle as he looks for more riders. If his minibus is near full, he'll be riding on the roof. We find small shops, and pick up enough food to hold us for the next several meals. A spectacular orange sunset lights up treetops and glass-sharded rooftops to the west.

~ ~ ~

Morning finds us back at Jorge Chavez Airport, boarding a flight bound for Cuzco. Once more, the people connections made at home through Elena have greased the wheels of the trip. She has contacted Margarita, a friend from years past. Margarita's daughter Chachi — who speaks English — meets us at the Cuzco airport and whisks us away to their home.

After warm introductions, a strange thing happens — they send us immediately to bed! "It's the altitude change," explains Chachi. "You've just flown from sea level to over 11,000 feet. You must rest and drink coca tea[3] to help your body acclimate." As if to emphasize the advice, four of the six of us are soon upset with nausea and headaches. Only Canyon and I (the youngest and oldest) remain comfortable, though we do rest with the others.

Nine-year-old Gustavo, Margarita's grandson, is in constant motion, dashing upstairs and down, bringing us coca tea and ice, and checking our chamber pots for freshness. Claudia, live-in student and house helper, is a huge help as well. By the next day, we're all on our feet again, feeling refreshed and much in debt to our hosts for their loving attention.

Margarita has plans for us. We will all travel together by taxi — she has a friend with a spacious one — into the Sacred Valley to experience the small town of Urubamba. Chachi will stay in Cuzco. Margarita speaks no English. Our Spanish consists of a smattering of words, though in a few years our children will all be capable of conversing in that language.

[3] The drinking of coca tea, and the chewing of coca leaves, for general health as well as to combat the effects of altitude on the human body, has been a practice for centuries among the people who dwell in the Andes of South America. Later, as we traveled to the Himalayas of India and Nepal, we used the prescription drug Diamox to prevent the onset of altitude sickness.

This is the land most dear to Margarita's heart. On the northern outskirts of Urubamba, behind the old adobe walls, lie rolling fields now planted in organic oregano for export. This was one of her projects, part of the outpouring of her life to help the farming families and children of the region. She shows us the orphanage she helped create and would have shared more of the history of her country and her work among the people. Language is the barrier, but her heart shows us more than her words ever could.

She has been waiting to bring us here — waiting all her life, it seems — to share these moments in her special place. When language fails, experience will be the teacher. Our family will remember these days for the rest of our lives.

The living is simple. We sleep on the concrete floor of a single small room. Meals are prepared and eaten in an equally tiny kitchen, the interior barely visible in the feeble light of a dim electric bulb that hangs

Gustavo and Claudia at home in Cuzco. The rabbits are not named — their destiny is the dinner table.

in a corner. The baño has no windows, no light, no toilet seat and no paper, but has been swept clean. It has an outside latch and the favorite trick of Marti Carmen, the resident 3-year-old, is to lock each of us in from the outside!

Margarita and her beloved Urubamba. The images are a product of our home darkroom, not Photoshop.

Marti Carmen's parents, Carlos and Matilda, live in a room beside the baño with Marti and her infant brother, Carlos Jr. Matilda chops firewood and cooks in an outdoor oven that resembles an inverted oversized hornets' nest. A Pepsi calendar of a bare-breasted maiden with drink in hand and a Shell Oil calendar of a young lady checking the oil while wearing only the bottom half of a string bikini dominate one wall. With a tranquil expression on his face, Jesus looks on from a frame on the opposite side of the room, a crucifix hanging nearby.

Eating is very basic. We have found some lentils and some rice. Potatoes, as for all the highland people, will be a mainstay. If we are to get greens into our diet, they must be soaked in iodine water for purification. But, whether we are in the center of Lima or in a remote Quechua village, pan (bread) is always available.

Pan usually takes the form of a small flat roll, five or six inches in diameter. They are sold ten for a sole — about four cents apiece and many times they will be our only food. We find that our four kids can devour twenty of them in an hour. One such morning comes and the bag is empty.

In a pouring rain at dawn I walk the mile into town, seeking out the poorer back streets as I have seen Margarita do. Here the pan is sold from doorways, in large wicker baskets covered with a cloth. I hop across the torrents and tightrope down the high curb, the narrow street taking on the appearance of a tributary of the Urubamba River.

I choose the middle doorway of the three pan sellers in the block, feeling that this one may be most in need, with the position of least business. A warm

Marti Carmen and friend at Urubamba.

smile and an "Hola!" greet me.

The bread has just been brought from the oven. As I step out of the doorway, a passing vehicle sends a wall of water my direction that soaks me from the waste down. But I see it coming and quickly shield my treasure. The bread is still dry and warm. I retrace my morning steps.

To the Incas, this valley was sacred. In rainy season it is dominated by the Urubamba River, and the town of Urubamba lies near the center of its forty-mile length. The surrounding mountains are hidden in clouds as the rain continues.

Their stomachs full of bread, the kids look for rainy-day pursuits. An hour or two is devoted to cards, but then the energy overflows. Forest and Gustavo engage in a friendly tussle, but when Gustavo's arm is pulled through his legs, he falls hard on the concrete, his head taking the entire impact.

I carry the listless figure to the sleeping room and check the pupils of his eyes for signs of concussion. There is rapid contraction of each pupil as my flashlight illuminates it. Good. But the swelling is evident and bruises are beginning to show.

Margarita has already sent for help. A thin, raggedly dressed older woman, of Quechua descent, hobbles through the gate on a deformed foot. Yet there is a calmness and radiance to her wrinkled face that belies the rest of her appearance. She kneels beside Gustavo and places her face close to the back of his head, which she cradles in her hands. For close to half an hour there is only the constant murmur of her voice.

"She is calling the spirit back," explains Margarita, and somehow we're able to understand. "The Inca believed that when a person was injured, his spirit partially left the body and needed to be restored."

By the time the woman is on her feet, so is Gustavo again, seemingly full of energy. Nevertheless, she will spend the next hour searching for, and gathering, various herbs. A poultice is made and applied to the side of Gustavo's face. By dinnertime, the poultice is removed and there is no sign of the injury — not even a bruise remains.

We ask Margarita for the name of the woman and she replies simply, "Llama Espiritual." We're not sure whether Margarita means that she is known as a shamaness or that her name is known only in the spiritual world. In any case, she is happy to join us for a dinner of asparagus soup over rice. We give her a few soles and a pack of needles. At the gate there is a mutual embrace. It is the only communication that any of us need.

~ ~ ~

Margarita — our guide and guardian — has brought us close to the earth and the people, made bargains we never could have, and in many ways cleared our path. She is with us at Pisac, Ollantaytambo, and Aguas Calientes. When I try to tell her that we will skip Machu Picchu because of the tourists and busyness, she clutches her hands to her heart and shakes her head.

Doug, Rivers, Trish, Autumn, Canyon, Margarita, Forest and Gustavo at Machu Picchu.

The day is late, so we all stay in Aguas Calientes, the small village at the base the great mountain whose summit is graced by Machu Picchu. We'll catch a morning train back to Cuzco. Here, we strike up an instant friendship with Ruth, a citizen of both Peru and

Canada, with her ready smile and gentle words in both Spanish and English.

But morning brings a surprise. During another night of heavy rain, a landslide has blocked the track that the local train must take, so there is only one train to bring out two trainloads of people. We are denied tickets. "If you can find a way to get on the train, you'll be OK," a policeman tells Ruth.

But at each car we try, the guard bars our way. A last minute negotiation between Ruth and one of the guards somehow opens the door — literally. The guard reaches down as the couplings begin to clank, the train lurches into motion and, amazingly, we are all hoisted aboard in the nick of time!

~ ~ ~

Margarita, whose presence has meant so much to us, must return to her home in Cuzco, and now our compass direction will be the result of our own choosing. We decide to head downriver to Ollantaytambo, this time by collectiva. For most of an hour, our driver negotiates a maze of potholes that require a series of sideways lurches, taking the shoulder on either side of the road. You get to know your fellow passengers well!

In the rainy season, the roads are strewn with boulders and sometimes blocked with mudslides. On our way from Urubamba to Ollantaytambo, we find the road almost totally blocked by a chunk of mountain the size of the collectiva. We barely squeeze between the rock and the roaring, flood-swollen river.

Ollantaytambo — the setting of Ethan Hubbard's first book of Peruvian adventures — is a good choice as we settle into the friendly hostel of Eva and Romulo for the next week. Their oldest son, José Luiz, is our guide each day as we hike to the Quechua village of Willoc, explore Puma Marca and trek to other lesser-known Inca ruins. Their daughter Yuditt has her 14th birthday and we are invited to the party. It's a great group of kids, and

Autumn keeps them laughing with her Appalachian clogging as her feet are flying in time to the Peruvian music.

With friends at Ollantaytambo: Back row: José Luiz, Yuditt, Autumn and Forest. Front row: Jón Luiz, Pamela, Canyon, Coré and Rivers.

The days in the village pass quickly, as we are always on the move, exploring trails, ruins or Quechua villages high in the Andes. One afternoon a woman arrives from Texas with half a dozen huge pieces of luggage. We find out that she has come to buy Quechua weavings, and in our minds we dismiss her as the typical U.S. tourist with more bags than she needs.

As we pass the courtyard where she's meeting with the weavers, we suddenly realize how far off the mark our own judgment has been. The many large suitcases are standing open, and contain not her belongings, but piles of donated clothing destined for the children in Willoc and other Quechua villages. We immediately feel the embarrassment of making a rash prejudgement.

~ ~ ~

As hard as it is to leave the Sacred Valley, we are drawn north by the Andean peaks of the Cordillera Blanca. After a never-ending, sleepless night in a long-distance bus, morning finds us blinking in the sunlight on the main street in the village of Hauraz. We find lodging for the night, stow our packs and take only the critical items with us.

No collectivas run the route we want, but there is a likely chance we can hitch a ride in the back of an open stake-bodied truck. And if the collectiva is the packed-in people experience, then the open truck is the next level of intimacy. Piled into the back with a dozen or so new acquaintances and their belongings, our 1960 vintage Dodge truck winds its way up, up into the Cordillera Blanca.

When we've finished a day-long, breathtaking hike along a glacier-fed creek, we flag a downhill truck, but we're late. Afternoon thunderstorms, followed by hail, have overtaken us. Everyone is grateful as the canvas cover is drawn over the back.

Could we live this way every day? Would we miss our personal vehicle and our high-speed highways? Of course. But we could live this life, too, you know. And we would find that, in its simplicity, the gifts of love — the kindness, the happiness — would be much more recognizable.

~ ~ ~

We are an American family in Peru. And though, in our month here, we have experienced what it is to miss meals and sleep on a concrete floor, we haven't really lived it. We know that in our pockets is the cash that can fill our stomachs with a good meal and the ticket that will take us safely home.

Although we are not considered wealthy in the United States, we are aware that our annual income is probably 15 times that of the Peruvian who considers himself well off.

Tonight we are still in Hauraz, near enough to the end of our trip that we know we can afford to eat in a restaurant. In fact, even with our family of six, there is food left over. We ask the restaurant folks to wrap it to go.

On the street it is pouring rain, and folks quickly scoot from the shelter of one doorway or overhang to another. The night is chilly, but our hi-tech raingear and warm layers keep us snug and warm. Our eyes sweep the street, alive with dancing puddles. There are many possibilities.

We decide on a group of three small children huddled against the wall on the opposite sidewalk. In a matter of seconds we are there.

One of the children, a girl of six or seven, starts to ask if we would like to buy a piece of candy or give a few centimos — we're not sure which.

For a moment her expression remains blank as we hand her half a pizza and a bowl of fettucini, still covered with wrapping. Then a light comes to her eyes that we will remember all our lives as she discovers the food and rushes to show her two friends. By the time we've re-crossed the street, the rare treat is already being devoured.

But there are tears in our eyes, as we know there are hundreds of others on the street whose night will be no different. And that there will be hundreds of other nights for those same children when no one will buy and no one will give and no one will care.

But for one brief moment, light has shown through the rain and we and the children have touched. They have taught us one more lesson in love, and it is for this that we are here.

~ ~ ~

At four, Canyon, our youngest, is a favorite with his golden hair, quick smile and the sparkle in his eyes. As we walk through any village, dozens of folks pass by with a smile and rumple his hair with their fingers. Quechua ladies at the corner catch him to their breasts with an "Ahh, niño" and other terms of endearment. His shy "Hola" and "Gracias" add to their delight.

Left, Quechua toddler at Aguas Calientes. Right, Canyon Sage at Ollantaytambo.

There are moments in which I feel vulnerable when walking the street alone. Yet I never feel safer than when I walk with my hand in that of our youngest Gringo niño. The experience of meeting the thief will not be ours this time.

~ ~ ~

Scenes that speak to our souls cry out at every turn. I finger the camera in my pocket, but hesitate.

There is the boy of seven or eight, nonchalantly peeing into the irrigation ditch. A hundred yards downstream, a young mother washes the family clothing in the same flow of water.

There are the girls of five or six, watching their sheep and pigs wander the roadside, searching for something to eat. An old man, bent with the toil of a lifetime, hauls one more load of firewood to town on his back. A teenage girl leads her donkeys to the river's edge to drink and shyly watches us from the shade of a nearby tree.

The tired Quechua woman who has worked the soil of her potato patch since dawn takes a moment to sit on a rock that was placed there centuries before. The time could have been 500 years earlier and her face could have looked exactly the same.

In a country where relatively few can afford the luxury of owning a camera, the difference between a camera-pointing tourist and the Peruvian who spends her entire day working to barely feed her children becomes sharply apparent.

We have learned, and perhaps it was intuitive before we even arrived, that we must spend time — a part of our own lives — sharing the day, eating the food, and carrying the burden of those whom we would like to call friend. Then, and only then, their eyes will reflect what we wish to see in our photograph.

So, for every scene that we capture, there will be a hundred that we pass. But those moments we carry with us too, forever etched in our hearts. And the images that do make it home reflect a bit of understanding shared between our lives and that of our new friends.

~ ~ ~

Someone asks if we had a spiritual experience in Peru. We pause to consider. If the question was intended to mean: Did we have a life-changing vision at the Sacred Rock of Machu Picchu or a heavenly intervention on the road to Damascus, then the answer would have to be "no."

But on the other hand, if the question meant: Was love at work on our journey? Did we touch — and were we touched by — the inner essence of those whom we met? Then the answer would certainly be "yes."

It might be in the eyes of the child with whom we shared our bread, or in the song of the Quechua woman that says simply that her life is whole. Or perhaps it is the smile and nod of the old man to whom we've shown a photo of our mountain valley at home. It is a hundred other hearts and hands — who call Peru home — who have reached out to help us on this journey.

We know, as we always have, that the greatest spiritual connection comes at ordinary times, in ordinary places and with ordinary people. But if we are to experience it, we must pause in our journey and recognize the times that our hearts are to give and the times when they must receive.

Choose Love, Not Fear

"Did I hear you correctly? You're going to take that darling little baby where? Guatemala? Chile? Peru?" "You might be robbed." "You won't be able to find the things you need." "She might be kidnapped." "Leave her with the grandparents. She won't remember the trip anyway. Wait 'til she's old enough to enjoy it." "Bicycling? Backpacking? Running a river? You are out of you mind!"

Those well-intentioned words of friends and relatives might make you feel that you were next of kin to Cruella DeVille, subjecting your children to untold punishment and hardship. Quite to the contrary, adventure travel in a new country — and interaction with folks from other cultures — when carried out with the needs of the youngest family members in mind, can be the peak experience of a lifetime.

Sure, there is extra planning and effort involved in making your adventure one which the children will enjoy and remember. But remember it they will, contrary to the misconceptions of many. Time and again, we have been amazed at this recall, even from a very young age. True, photos and family tales reinforce this memory, but there is a reservoir of actual experience building in every young mind.

Trish and I feel that it is essential that our children come to know how most of the world lives, the differences from, and similarities to, our own lives. This means *really connecting* — being on foot, on a bicycle, or riding a local bus, where we make eye contact and exchange a few words with those whose world we've entered. It means living with families, often in rudimentary accommodations, sleeping and eating as they do, and sharing their chores and projects as the opportunity arises. In many ways, this is not difficult for us, since we can't afford the usual tourist amenities anyhow.

But tent camping also brought us close to those from whom we had come to learn. We might find our tents surrounded by curious kids, waiting for a glimpse of our family or to try out a few words of English with us. Every campground has a fútbol (soccer) field, where all are welcome in pickup games — a great place to make new friends!

Not everyone goes to school in Miss Frizell's magic yellow bus, but this Delhi, India bus surely must have magic of its own!

Children are the key to a very different, much more rewarding, type of travel experience — they open doors. When we are observed in a faraway place, or doing something unusual in the company of kids, folks that see us will often start a conversation or invite us to share their home where that would never have happened had we simply been two traveling adults.

Our kids have found similarities between themselves and their new friends, quite apart from the circumstances which dictate those friends' living conditions. In other words, we try to see that their young minds gain experience in connecting from the heart before judgments and prejudice take hold.

They have found that those with the fewest possessions are often the ones that most want to give of the little they have. A meal. The most comfortable place to sleep. Any bit of hospitality to add to your comfort. Our own young ones have seen a reason for learning another language. They have learned to wash clothes in a bucket or creek and hang them on bushes to dry, simply because there is no other choice and it's the way it's done there.

As the years passed by, and each child reached her or his teen years, it became apparent that they had acquired the confidence of seasoned travelers. There was no hesitation in traveling alone, often into countries where a language other than English was spoken. They have never lost the ability to evaluate and change direction if a scary situation demanded it. But initially, they reach out with a natural friendliness and trust to all whom they meet. Misconception and fear have vanished and been replaced with understanding and love.

And, no, parents don't have all the answers — they just may learn as much as the kids in these situations! And when we look back, we find that these adventures have been the most meaningful educational experiences in all of our lives.

~ ~ ~

Having taken charge of the "time factor" in your life — whether by extended, unpaid time away from your job, a sabbatical, work that allows a season of choice, or a major shift in your lifestyle — you have created an unparalleled learning opportunity for you and your children. Don't waste it. Pull out the map. Plan the adventure. Grab your pack. Go!

You are taking your kids into the greatest of all classrooms — one that needs no designated schedule, desks or lesson plans. One that has unlimited possibilities.

The teachers will be many. Some will be as young as your little ones — some even younger. Others might be gray-haired, offering you fresh baked bread, a jewel of wisdom, or perhaps just a smile. Your kids will make connections of their own through games and play. They will see reasons for learning another language as they keep their friendships alive through letters or email.

In Chitwan, Nepal, Canyon feeds bananas to the bull elephant that Autumn was later instrumental in rescuing.

Traveling in Nepal, however, brought us close to species we had never before encountered. Curiosity was difficult to contain, and Canyon decided that he would not be happy until he had ridden a camel. There was, of course, a camel-handler willing to oblige.

What Canyon found, on his way to the village astride his dromedary, was that camels and elephants don't really care for each other. When his camel would pass an elephant, the camel would hiss, spit, and sidestep, while each elephant would stomp the ground and make guttural complaints. Fortunately, the hostility was limited to body language, and did not escalate into physical contact!

Much more meaningful, however, was an elephant encounter that opened all of our eyes to the treatment that these intelligent and majestic animals often receive in captivity. A bull elephant, the tallest in a group of 15 or 20, had what appeared to be a saddle-sore between the tourist box and the spot behind, where the handler sat. The appalling truth soon jumped out at us — that this fist-sized crater never healed — it was akin to an "accelerator pedal," the handler's stick being jabbed into the elephant's open flesh every 30 seconds or so while on a forest walk, causing the giant to run in excruciating pain.

You could see his agony as he ran almost blindly after each jab — also the smile on his face as he was fed bananas by Canyon. Autumn took a photo of him, found a Nepalese large animal rescue agency online, and based on her description and letters, within a year she received word at home that they had taken the elephant from his owners and placed him in a "retirement area."

~ ~ ~

Ladakh had been its own kingdom for more than 2,000 years before becoming part of India in its northernmost reaches. Its villages and Buddhist monasteries are tiny green dots in the most barren parts of the Himalayas. The people of these villages have been self-sufficient for untold centuries, but this is changing as climate change shrinks the life-giving glaciers, and the Western ways of marketing and consumption tempt the young folks to migrate to the cities, causing a labor scarcity at home.

With water channeled from faraway glaciers through ancient sluiceways, barley is grown in every village. It is this crop that sustains the inhabitants through the -40°F winters, and the collected dung of all village animals that provides heat for their homes.

Our family was there in the village of Phyang at barley harvest time, able to carry and stack bundles from the fields, but not nearly skilled enough to efficiently help with the cutting or threshing. We watched, learned, and gained great appreciation for the traditions that are passed from generation to generation, knowledge that has enabled these mountain folk to flourish without outside help for so many centuries. During the time we were guests in her home, Yong Dol, mother of three, amazed us with the variety of mouthwatering foods that could be produced from a handful of basic ingredients.

Canyon carrying a barley bundle at harvest time in Phyang, Ladakh.

We learned much from our time in Yong Dol's home, where her children and husband's parents lived in an extended family relationship, a rarity in the United States. Being a Buddhist household, prayer flags fluttered from the roof and our meals were eaten from a low table while we sat on the floor, ornate kettles of ancient vintage glowing from shelves surrounding the dung stove. Yak butter and butter tea were daily staples of the Chirpon family and their guests.

All water comes from the glaciers high in the Himalayas, greening the valleys through which it passes. Unfortunately, global warming is melting these glaciers to a degree where they may no longer sustain life. We washed our clothing in the same manner that Yong Dol did — on a stone pedestal fifty feet below the house. Showering was done in a small nearby enclosure by pouring a bucket of frigid water over our heads, the grandmother popping in, mid-shower, to see if we needed soap!

Eating dinner with the extended family in the Chirpon home in the village of Phyang in Ladakh.

Monks dancing at the Phyang Monastery.

Too soon, we took leave of our Ladakh friends, and boarded the remains (broken windshield, hard, mismatched seats) of what was once a decent bus, for the two-day trip from Leh to Manali over the second-highest motor road in the world. Every two hours, the bus would grind to a halt and the passengers would dash a short distance away to do their personal business.

It seemed impossible that two vehicles could meet and pass on this narrow road, and I would swear that our wheels were hanging over the edge when we did. The occasional carcasses of tractor trailers and busses in the gorges far below confirmed that not all attempts at passing were successful.

Late in the afternoon of our second day in the bus we descended into Manali, where we were able to engage a taxi for the climb to Dharamsala and McLeod Ganj, the home of the Dalai Lama in exile from Tibet. We found two rooms in the Geden Choeling Convent and soon learned to keep our doors — and windows — closed at all times to prevent the ever-present monkeys from pilfering our food and belongings.

Trish had been here three years earlier and become good friends with Yang Zom, a nun with a hair-raising story of escape from Chinese-occupied Tibet during winter, the only one in her group of nine nuns to make it over the snow-covered passes that season. Several years after our family visit to McLeod Ganj, we learn that she has left the convent, married and given birth to a son. When Yang Zom is later able to visit the United States, we get to meet her husband and young son, spending time with them and continuing our friendship.

Virtually all of the nuns at Geden Choeling are refugees from the Chinese occupation of Tibet, each with her own story to tell. We get to know a bit about life at the convent, and contemplate the tragic display outside of the Dalai Lama's home of several hundred photos of monks who have committed suicide by self-immolation in protest of the Chinese repression in their country. On our last full day, we hike high into the cloud-shrouded mountains above McLeod Ganj, into a solitude interrupted only by the passing of a farmer and his plodding yak on the steep trail.

~ ~ ~

With vivid memories of friends made and bustling life in McLeod Ganj, we turn south, leaving the calming embrace of the Himalayas as an overnight bus promises to get us to Delhi by morning. Never trust the promise of a bus in India! Sometime in the dark of night, we pull into a dimly lit roadside shed where there is much metal-to-metal hammering for an hour.

Apparently repaired from a malady unrevealed to us, the bus groans back onto the road, making headway until about an hour before dawn when it suddenly limps unevenly onto the grassy shoulder. Flat tire. Not having a jack to raise the rear of the bus seems to present no problem as long as the driver has a shovel. Fortunately the flat is in the outside tire of the dual wheel and the driver simply digs a pit beneath it while the inside wheel supports the bus.

Having no spare — of course! — the bus driver sends the errant wheel off in the wire basket of a passing cycle-rickshaw, the peddler being almost obscured by the giant wheel. We wait nearly two hours, with no visible progress on the repair and return of the errant wheel. Running out of time in our own schedule, we're able to hail a passing taxi and make it to the Delhi Airport just in time for our flight to Pune.

We'll be staying several nights with the Bankar family at their home in Pune. One of their daughters, Rujuta, spent a year as a high school exchange student in our hometown of Franklin, where we enjoyed introducing her to the trails and rivers of the southern Appalachians. After some initial hesitation, we've cautiously invited ourselves to be guests of Rujuta's family.

At the Pune Airport, all of our uncertainty quickly vanishes. The entire family — Rujuta and her parents, with sister Vedashree — are on hand to welcome us with smiling faces, hugs and flowers. Rather than taking us to their home, however, we are immediately whisked into the midst of the Ganesh[4] Festival, tens of thousands of moving, celebrating revelers packing the streets so tightly that if you lost your balance, you would likely stay upright.

Getting separated from our hosts in such a crowd is a frightening prospect. But through hours of walking, dancing and sudden dashes to keep up, passing one elaborate Ganesh display after another, we are still with them. Their destination is a part of the celebration that is off limits to most of the crowds, but somehow we are designated "honored guests" and brought to the well-guarded display of ancient golden Ganesh relics, where we are presented with scarves and scrolls describing the meaning of this festivity.

Rujuta and Vedashree smile in front of Ganesh, the elephant-headed god of good fortune and success.

At last we are taken to the Bankar family home, where we are again welcomed like royalty, Nuton, Rujuta and Vedashree's mother,

4 Ganesh is the Hindu god with elephant head and human body, who is said to provide prosperity, good fortune and success. He is the Lord of Beginnings and the Remover of Obstacles, both material and spiritual. The principle qualities of the elephant are wisdom and effortlessness.

carefully marking the center of our foreheads with the red dot signifying that we are honored guests in the Hindu tradition.

We sleep at the comfortable, temporarily vacant apartment of friends of their family, but eat delicious meals with the Bankars themselves. In their home, meals are taken Hindu style while seated on the floor, using fingers for serving and eating. When we take them out to eat, they introduce us to dosas[5] which are a huge hit with our family, particularly Canyon, who is determined to find a way to open a dosa shop upon his return to the States.

Canyon, about to devour a dessert dosa. By the time we had left Pune, he had learned how to make them.

While we are in their part of India, the Bankars give more than we can ever repay, filling every moment with new experiences, as well as insights into the history and culture which mean so much to them. The parents drive us to Mumbai, the city of their youth, where we wander among the open-air markets, attempt to comprehend the heartbreaking poverty of millions and at last relax among some boulders along the waterfront. It is an experience that Canyon will write about in his college entrance essays.

[5] The dosa is a very thin, large-diameter pancake, the batter being made from rice and mungo beans. It can be filled with any of a huge variety of tasty vegetable or dessert recipes.

On another day, the women of the family will take us by taxi, two hours to Aurangabad and thence to the Buddhist caves of Ajanta — a mind-boggling array of 30 massive caves, hollowed out 100 years BC. Six hundred subsequent years of carving on the interior walls and columns has made the complex into a spectacular display of history and art. We are awed by what lies within this mountain of granite.

Our interaction with this lovely family, the awareness of the many small acts of kindness between us, and the growing friendship between Canyon and Vedashree — the pair are close to the same age, each looking toward college and very much enjoying each other's company — all make it difficult to leave. But of course the day comes and with many hugs and promises to meet again, we move on to the next chapter of our lives, with vivid memories to shed light on our future paths.

~ ~ ~

"And just how, even as homeschoolers, do you handle all that time away from home and the kids' missing their studies?" you might ask. When we venture into cultures different from our own, do our children take school books with them? Rarely — and not really necessary. The interaction with new friends and the exposure to different ways of life has been their (and our) primary learning experience.

But we most definitely encourage them to keep journals — they will be invaluable as the years pass. If the kids are too young to journal on their own, we have them take ten or fifteen minutes each day to dictate to us those sights and happenings that have most impressed them. And, of course, we keep our own journals.

Those that we meet always want to see what our lives are like. A small book with photos showing our home, chores, fun activities, pets, favorite places nearby and more transcends language barriers and creates a bond with those whose lives we've entered.

Above all, we try to remember that we are there to learn and be a part of the experience that we are observing. If we isolate our family in an expensive hotel or behind the tinted windows of a fancy automobile, we would not experience the friendships and lessons for which we came.

Initially we spent time in several English-speaking countries, however, most of our journeys have been to countries south of the United States — Guatemala, Peru, Chile, Costa Rica, Panama, Mexico — though India and Nepal have given us much as well. As our children grew older, they added to this list through their own individual travels — Haiti, Nicaragua, Argentina, Uruguay, Brazil, Honduras, El Salvador, China, France, Ireland.

When it's too far to walk, you take a chicken bus. Pokara, Nepal

We have always refused to call the poorer countries (in material wealth only) by the commonly used elitist terms. One of the major lessons that we all learn from time spent there is that the majority of the world labors much harder than we do in the U.S., for a tiny fraction of the return. Yet, for all this material poverty there is a richness of spirit that reaches out to others, and most are ready to share the little that they have with their guests.

When visiting our neighbors in countries with a simpler lifestyle, we live, when possible, with a family, eating what they eat and sleeping under the same thatched or tin roof. And, of course, paying our own way, so that we're not a burden added to their marginal lifestyle.

If we change locations, we'll ride the "chicken buses," ancient retired U.S. school buses, so named for the baskets of chickens often secured to the roof. We might use a "squat-hole" or a toilet without a seat. And if there is a sewerage system at all, it is not designed to handle toilet paper — that goes into the waste basket, that is, if you've brought paper of your own.

And what kind of an image will your family project as you make new friends? Though these friends will want to know what your life is like back home, it's not necessary to bring it all along with you. Traveling simply, with a single backpack, can provide your personal necessities, yet tells the world you're a savvy traveler, as well as counteracting the "wealthy American tourist" image.

The younger your children, however, the more you as parents add to your own load and there are circumstances where an additional bag will be necessary to carry diapers, snacks, special books and other items necessary for your child's happiness and comfort.

The days spent in sharing the lives of those who at first appear so different from ourselves have been some of the most meaningful educational experiences of our children's lives. And there is little doubt that the same is true for us as parents.

As Wade Davis has so eloquently said:

The world in which you were born is just one model of reality. Other cultures are not failed attempts at being you: They are unique manifestations of the human spirit.

Buddhist prayer flags await the breeze on a rooftop in Phyang, Ladakh, the village monastery visible on the far ridge. Muslim and Buddhist families live in harmony in this Himalayan village, as they have for over 2,000 years. The fodder in the foreground will be tossed down to feed yaks and goats who live under the family home during the bitter winters.

Wilderness Challenges

Our family has found that time in the wilderness takes us away from the artificial, and sometimes frantic, rhythms of "civilized" life so that what is happening around us is simply the flow of the natural world as it interacts with all of its parts. I think that is the factor that so refreshes our spirit — not to mention our body — when we spend extended time on a wilderness river or trail. It is then that we realize that we are not just immersed in the world of nature, but that we are, and always will be, a part of, and dependent on it.

Trish and I, before we met in 1979, both traveled trails and rivers that took us into wilderness, often for extended periods of time. It was only natural that we would continue this as partners. When I say "wilderness," I mean not just the areas on a map which are officially designated as such, but also those smaller, more intimate pockets — often tucked away for one reason or another — where humans have not interfered with the natural balance.

Sure, as adults experienced in outdoor adventure, we were capable as a pair, but what happens as we become parents? Could we introduce small children, even infants, to wilderness, and why in the world would we? Assuming this was a rational desire, and would benefit the child both now and in her future, how should we do it?

From the time Autumn was a few months old, she became a tiny passenger on our bike touring trips. We would pedal all over the mountains of home, through fall foliage, alongside rushing creeks, camping at favorite spots, particularly those with children's playgrounds and gentle beaches by water. Even before she

could walk, Autumn had savored the trails of our home mountains from the vantage point of Mom or Dad's shoulders; or been
a crew member in our open canoe, dipping her tiny paddle into
the water as her parents navigated a mild whitewater river.

As each child matured, so also did the awareness of wild country
and her or his relationship to it. As a toddler, a campfire was
intriguing and adding sticks to the flames made the child feel a
useful part of the experience. A year or two later, that same child
would know where on a pine tree to find dry kindling, even in
rain or snow. How to build and light the fire. With the passing of
a few more years, where to place a fire, how to safely contain it,
and the judgment to not build a fire in windy or dry conditions
would become part of the skill set.

At age 5, Canyon takes a turn at the oars in a calm section of Utah's Green
River. September, 1998

The same could be said for scores of minor or major decisions on
trails, rivers and bike trips as each child grew in proficiency. There
was a burning desire to reach — or surpass — the competency of
Mom, Dad or the older siblings in any of the outdoor activities in
which the family might immerse itself.

When Canyon arrived, he was, at seven months of age, one of the
youngest ever to run the Gates of Lodore section of the Green

River. It was a week-long trip, and one on which we did exercise some prudence in carrying him around Upper Disaster Falls — where John Wesley Powell lost the dory, No Name — and the intimidating Hell's Half Mile, which takes all of our skill to avoid wrapping the raft around the boulder in the main chute.

Dozens of adventures later — on challenging rivers and steep trails — the kids matured as experienced wilderness persons in their own right. All have become competent kayakers on challenging whitewater rivers, often working seasonal jobs as rafting guides. Each has become a Wilderness First Responder when the time was right, a skill considered vital for outdoor leaders.

~ ~ ~

But let's backtrack a decade or so. Trish and I were not the only ones in the family to share their woodsy skills with our younger four. My two older children, so dear to my heart, were, and are, very much immersed in outdoor experiences. Cricket and David, as toddlers, often sat just in front of me in the cockpit of my white-water kayak — one at a time and with appropriate life jacket, of course — as I would eddy-hop upstream in a long Class 3 (medium difficulty) rapid. After ten minutes of hard work, we would lean, turn and enjoy the wild downstream ride.

A few years later, they were each paddling junior-sized fiberglass kayaks, boats created in our basement workshop with the help of their own hands. We enjoyed lake paddling together as I brought food and camping gear in an open canoe, mild whitewater rivers, and weekend backpacking trips. Then came the call of the remote North Country. Alaska. The big adventure.

The Far North

Barely into their teens, Cricket and Dave tackle a 430-mile adventure, 100 miles north of the Arctic Circle, on Alaska's Noatak River.

"You've got to come to Alaska," Joe urged. "The best wilderness rivers you'll ever kayak are up here. Bring Cricket and Dave and we'll all run the Noatak this summer. I think I can even find boats for you in Kotzebue."

My friend Joe Terrell had been working out of Kotzebue, Alaska, a hundred miles north of the Arctic Circle for the past four years. His offer was tempting, and the thought of that wild and long a river adventure immediately raised my excitement level.

I ordered sectional topographic maps — there were no large-scale maps of that region — and spent evenings studying the river and the surrounding country. I talked about the expedition with

Cricket and Dave as we devoured books that brought to life the Alaskan North Country. My three weeks of vacation were appropriately scheduled for late July and early August.

I called Joe on his satellite phone in Kotzebue to tell him the good news. There was an uncharacteristic period of silence before he spoke.

"Uh, Doug … there's something you should know. I can't go with you. A job has just come up at King Cove out in the Aleutians, too big a job to pass up."

"Oh."

"But the three of you can still paddle the Noatak. I'll find the boats for you up here. You can sleep and eat in the construction trailer and Cliff Hyatt will arrange for your bush flight."

"That sounds workable, but we're sure going to miss you."

"I might see you at the end of your trip."

Not even underway, our adventure had suddenly taken an unexpected turn.

Joe had not run the Noatak himself, but knew a few who had. He passed on what information he could. Our trip would be over four hundred miles long and in tundra north of the timberline for the most part. It was now the rainy season. The river had no rapids rated higher than a Class III. There would be abundant wildlife and the possibility of bear encounters. We were warned to keep our camp and clothing free of food odors, particularly fish.

There was no human habitation anywhere near our route with the exception of a tiny Inuit village about fifty miles from the mouth of the river. No one would come looking for us until we were at least a week overdue. It was the summer of 1978 and we were on our own.

There was no hesitation among the three of us — it was going to be an adventure worthy of a Tolkien tale. Hopefully without the trolls! Tickets were booked. Clothing, food and gear were carefully planned, assigned to specific waterproof river bags and prepacked. We were on our way to the far north!

In that year, U.S. time zones had not yet been consolidated; in Kotzebue we were a long six hours west of our Atlanta starting time. Having arrived in that tiny village, the lengthy day of arctic summer gave us the feeling that we had no sleeping time at all. Nevertheless, following only a few hours of shuteye, morning found us awake and scrambling to transfer our food and gear to waterproof river bags and get all to the airstrip.

The mood at Baker Aviation was somber. The previous day they had lost their other Cessna 185 and pilot, Jeff, when he flew into a mountainside in bad weather, just east of the continental divide and Noatak headwaters.

Our pilot, Greg, looks at our gear and shakes his head, but somehow it stows behind the seats, with only a kayak left over to ride on Cricket and Dave's laps!

"If the 185, with the three of you and all that gear, can make it into the air, I'll get you to the river," quips Greg, and we wonder how serious he is about this being a marginal take-off. Ten minutes later, the Cessna claws its way off the runway and into a rainy morning.

The weather is low, with a ceiling of 1100 feet, drizzling continuously, as we hop across ten miles of ocean to the mouth of the Noatak River and its impressive delta. From here, we snake our way along the twisting river, taking shortcuts over mountains, often no more than fifty feet off the ground to avoid the clouds.

Greg would like to land us at the junction of the Noatak and Cutler Rivers, since he has never flown beyond that point. However, that would put us about eighty miles short of the high mountains and what we feel will be one of the most beautiful parts of the trip. He hands me the map and asks me to pick out landmarks as he keeps the plane buzzing upriver.

Greg flies on, but of course the final decision will be his — we're flying with wheels, not pontoons, and will have to find a suitable gravel bar for landing. The valley begins to narrow as the mountain walls become more impressive.

Pilot error in Alaska often has fatal consequences. Fortunately, all in this DeHaviland Beaver survived the crash.

At a bend just below Otkurak Creek, we catch a glimpse of brilliant blue. We figure that it must be the tent of another river group. But as we fly closer, we see it's not a tent but a downed plane.

Greg puts the Cessna into a tight spiral and we drop quickly, making several passes just over the wreck. He remembers now that a DeHaviland Beaver — which this is — went down on the Noatak a week ago. Overloaded, it tried to take off from the gravel bar and couldn't clear the riverbank, plowing into the tundra and breaking apart without a fire. No one was killed.

We fly on, rain pounding the windshield and ragged clouds filling the valley. We're almost to the river's source as the glaciers on Mt. Igikpak suddenly appear through a break in the clouds.

"Far enough," says Greg, and puts the Cessna into a 180 degree turn to look for a suitable gravel bar. Most are small or irregular, but finally one meets with his approval. We make two trial passes and on the third, despite the choppy wind and rain, Greg sets the load down as easily as a mosquito landing on your hand.

We quickly unload, Greg taxies to the end of the bar, waves, and is airborne. For what seems an interminable time, he flies straight at the dark mountainside which marks the western end of the intimidating Brooks Range, gaining airspeed, and at the last second pulls up and banks to the right. A wiggle of wings and he's gone.

Our bush pilot leaves the three of us on a gravel bar island in Alaska's Brooks Range, far from human habitation. Ahead of us lies a sixteen-day odyssey on the Noatak River, covering 430 river and ocean miles, ending at the village of Kotzebue, just east of the Bering Sea.

We are alone on a gravel island, over 400 miles from the nearest human habitation. Whatever we have with us must suffice for the next two to three weeks. Joe has graciously loaned us two boats, and his friend Cliff a third. Two are inflatable kayaks (German Metzelers) and the third is a two-person Folboat. We spend the next two hours assembling and inflating, as the case may be.

After a few "selfies by tripod" in the drizzle, we stow the camera, load the kayaks and shove off. I'm paddling the "barge" (the Folboat with most of the gear — probably 300 lbs!) and Cricket and Dave, the inflatables, with what pieces could fit into their limited space.

We're still feeling the shift to Bering Standard Time, so we make camp early after stopping to investigate the downed plane. The river current is strong, but no rapids yet, making the paddling easy.

Camp is set up in a grassy tundra area on the south bank — actually a little bit marshy. Mosquitoes are out in force and the bush hats with netting are life-savers. Clouds begin breaking up in early evening and by 8pm it is definitely clearing. Sunset begins about 10:30pm and lingers as the evening becomes chilly. We fry up a delicious salmon given to us by Jan, who cooks for the construction crew back in Kotzebue. She was delighted by a gallon of Tupelo honey that we left for her.

~ ~ ~

Early morning clouds on the mountains soon give way to sunshine and brilliant blue skies. A small taffy-colored animal works its way along the far riverbank — about the size of a marmot. It *is* a marmot! Moments later, a red fox (arctic foxes are blue or white) makes an appearance in the same area.

The river level has fallen almost a foot — we don't know yet whether this is a daily cycle from the snowmelt or a permanent drop following the rain. If it stays down, it will probably mean trouble for the heavily loaded Folboat on the shallow gravel bars.

Cricket comments on the effect of solitude on the mind and how sometimes we concentrate on the smaller details of the day. She and Dave have each memorized the warning label on the shaft of their paddles while I've kept track of my ongoing battle with mosquitoes. The Bite/Swat score: Mosquitoes: 83, Dad: 11.

~ ~ ~

We wake up several times — to bright sunlight at 4am, and again about every hour. I'm up at 8am, letting Cricket and Dave sleep until nine. The water level has dropped another three inches, so we're evidently losing the rain effect.

As we pass the junctions of the Kugrak and Igning rivers, we have the choice of taking dozens of water channels, some not rejoining others for half a mile or more. About noon, we paddle down on a caribou swimming the river from the south to north bank, head and antlers held impressively above the water. He then turns and trots toward us along the north shore after a vigorous shaking. I take a quick shot with the 50mm lens, then scramble for the telephoto, losing my lens cap to the river. The caribou takes an amazed look at us and is gone.

Tonight, we make camp on a sandy bar on the south shore with a stand of glowing green grass, usually seen only in springtime. The place is evidently a favorite of others, too — we pick out the tracks of bear and wolf, as well as many smaller animals. Some large leg bones lie in the sand.

~ ~ ~

Today we cover 15 to 20 miles, the best yet, but still below our required average of 25 to 30. Taking it slow to enjoy the high country and get the muscles used to paddling is probably the best bet at the beginning.

We treat David's thumb, as we have each evening, with alcohol and anti-biotic ointment. David cut his thumb rather badly in Kotzebue just before we left. The spot where the flesh is missing, about as big as a fingernail, is looking better — no sign of infection.

In mid-afternoon we sight an unusual looking object in the middle of the river far downstream. Unusual, because the river is very predictable so far, without rapids or large rocks, just gravel bars and strong currents.

But as we come closer, we can see the fuselage of another bush plane — upside down with the tail and wings visible beneath the water. It's in line with a long gravel bar that appears good enough for take-off and landing, but obviously was not — at least for this pilot! This crash looks older than the first — but hard to tell, being in the river. I wonder about the life expectancy of a bush pilot.

We stop for lunch on a gravel bar, skinny-dipping and rock hunting. There is such variety and beauty, even in tiny pebbles, making us wonder about the origin of each. Every day, we add a few (or more than a few) to our load, at a very minimum replacing the weight of food eaten with the new ballast.

~ ~ ~

We're underway at 11:15am. Mornings are still slow. We paddle three hours before eating lunch, but with the Folboat we can nibble on snacks as we paddle, since food can be easily accessed in the cockpit.

Rocks are larger now — one and two feet in diameter — and I have to be even more precise with navigation to avoid damage to the Folboat skin. Many marmots watch our river passage with interest and I pull ashore, trying to creep up on a caribou for a photo. I don't get very close, but pick a handful of blueberries before returning to the boats.

By noon it starts to rain and stays with us off and on for the rest of the day. We surprise several caribou on a sandbar and they bolt away on thundering hooves.

Just beyond the sandbar, we find that Midas Creek loops around to almost touch the Noatak before actually joining it a mile downstream. Paddling in the rear, Cricket is viewed for a long while by a curious red fox keeping pace with us along the riverbank.

There's a brief break in the weather, so we make camp, cook dinner and climb into the tent, snuggling into our bags. The rain settles down in earnest.

~ ~ ~

The light never goes out! Three in the morning and it's bright enough to wake up. But the pouring rain continues, causing us to just snuggle down tighter in our sleeping bags. Finally it subsides about 9:30 am. and we start the morning chores. A reprieve this morning, but later on, we may have to pack up in the early rain in order to make our daily mileage.

Winding through a miniature canyon with hills and moraine slides on each side, we find ourselves in a series of Class 2 rapids. No sweat for the decked boats, once Cricket decides to wear her spray skirt, but I've got to take great pains to keep the barge away from the largest standing waves.

More caribou and marmots appear on the banks. Arctic terns dart here and there, then hover in one spot over the water, flapping their wings rapidly, like a hummingbird. Toward evening a cormorant flies over with a fish in its mouth.

Right after lunch we pass a mother and two young loons that keep diving to avoid our seeing them. Finally, the mother and one chick go upstream, the other, likely quite terrified, heading off alone in the opposite direction.

By late afternoon, as we're beginning to come out of the mountains, we run smack into fierce headwinds with a 50°F air temperature. Without trees or hills, there's no chance for a windbreak and camp is made early near a gravel bar — on the north shore for the first time.

What a treat is in store as we sit by our campfire eating. First one, then two, and finally three red foxes appear to put on a show for us, dancing and leaping on the gravel bar, pausing to sit and observe us from 150 ft away, all the while barking and wailing plaintively. Years later, Cricket commented, "I love this memory so much. I can still see them in the low blue light of continuous dusk."

~ ~ ~

Sleep seems so necessary — we can't help but get nine or ten hours a night — so no early start today. We leave at 11am, not early, but it's the best yet for us, and paddle until 8pm, with a 45-minute lunch stop.

Today is caribou day! Lone bulls against the skyline are the first seen, then small herds of eight or ten, crossing the river at several places. Finally, a herd of about fifty appears at a spot that looks perfect for camping. They disappear up the bank and over the bluff as we put ashore.

We vie for a camping spot with a curious caribou herd.

Then an amazing thing happens. A second caribou herd starts grazing down the shore, completely unaware of our presence since we are standing downwind of them and against the setting sun. We freeze in place — except for the camera — and the herd walks right into our camp. They surround us as they graze, before finally realizing something is different and bounding out of sight.

Cricket's feelings speak for us all. "What I remember best about this is that the big bucks were first, and so they got the closest. And that it's one thing to see them from afar and quite another to be close enough to hear the click of their feet and hear them breathing, and to realize how very big they are. My heart was pounding!"

This is the second day in a row that we've seen no bush planes — just a lone seagull that had a lot to say to us. It's our best paddling day yet for distance — all three of us stuck together pretty well and covered 25 to 30 miles.

There are large bear tracks in the sand, about a day old. It's a cold, cold evening with snow on the riverbank at one spot, a beautiful sunset and a warm campfire. All is peaceful at Caribou Gardens.

~ ~ ~

And an even colder night — below freezing — keeps us snuggled deep into our sleeping bags in the morning until the sun can warm the tent. We pay for it with a late start, as we hit the river at noon.

The day is good for paddling — sunny with fast-moving clouds racing by, but only a light wind on the river — that is, until about 6pm, when a stiff, cold north wind comes up. At 8pm we pass the junction of the Cutler River and camp an hour later on the north shore, at a place shielded from the wind. Looks like another cold night, though — air temperature is already at 42° F.

All day we have seen caribou — in small groups or medium

herds — in fact, we woke to a bunch grazing right next to us again at our Caribou Gardens site. Many caribou are swimming the river in groups and one keeps coming up to look us over from the beach as we enjoy a chilly morning dip in the river.

No people, no bush planes today. We have our best paddling day yet, putting more than 30 miles under our kayaks. Another fabulous sunset wows us, as half the sky is a sweeping salmon-colored cloud culminating in bright gold light around the sun. The wide-angle lens can't begin to take it all in.

Cricket and Dave are exhausted as usual, skipping both back rubs and reading.

~ ~ ~

A steady patter of rain on the tent wakes us in the morning after that beautiful sunset last night. No fair! We try to out-sleep it, but to no avail as we finally arise, eat breakfast and pack in the rain. Even the mosquitoes are still active, despite the wet.

The rain eases in the early afternoon, but the heavy steel-gray clouds follow us all day and evening. It's another long paddling day of over 30 miles — we pass the Anisak River and start looking for a campsite, rejecting five in the process, including a beach with huge fresh bear tracks.

By the time we find a suitable site — with smaller bear tracks — it's after 10pm. A fox has followed us along the bank for over half a mile, just looking us over as we search for a campsite. We finally pick a sandy spot, not having found a grassy one.

Very strange, but ever since we passed the Cutler River last evening, we have not seen a single caribou — as if they have an imaginary boundary! Again, no people or bush planes today.

Toward evening, we see our first trees of the trip — a small grove of twelve-foot cottonwoods on the north shore.

~ ~ ~

After waking late, with full sun on the tent, we spread gear out to dry so we can shake out the sand and make a clean start — more or less.

The Folboat develops a small leak — about two gallons an hour — right at the stern wear point. As we come ashore for lunch, the skin and frame structure is quickly unloaded, we dry the leaking area and apply a vulcanizing patch. Carefully setting the boat back in the river without dragging, we reload the gear. The skin appears to be watertight once more.

Again, we don't see a caribou all day. Also, no people, no bush planes. Generally, we have a north wind — it wants to blow us off the river on the east to west legs of the hairpin turns.

We pick a south shore campsite by a tributary creek and are immediately greeted by a fox, who sniffs the tent and kayaks as we are assembling camp, and seems eager to sniff us if given the chance! The fox just sits and watches from various vantages, then takes a ten-foot leap over the creek and is gone.

~ ~ ~

We're seeing more and more trees now — all cottonwoods, all near the river and all under 15 feet tall. A golden eagle soars majestically along our route, stopping just for a moment on its nest atop the cliffs north of Isaoktuvik Creek.

From our campsite of last night to the start of the Grand Canyon of the Noatak, we've noticed a strange noise on the surface of the water — like CO_2 bubbles when a soft drink has been opened. Under close inspection, you can actually see tiny bubbles rising, but not obvious on the surface. This occurs for perhaps a couple of hundred yards, then again a mile or so later. There must be some kind of gas being released through the river bottom.

We've also encountered quicksand at a number of places on the trip, usually where a small creek joins the river. The sand nearby may be very firm, and then all of a sudden the whole surface is quivery and liquid-like. Boots tend to disappear quickly and it can be a tough retrieval if the foot is loose. We've noticed also, from their tracks, that bears never walk in the quicksand!

Evening finds us three quarters of the way through the Grand Canyon of the Noatak, which so far isn't much like a canyon at all. Rumors of rapids here appear unfounded, as we have not encountered anything better than a Class 1. This has been the most favorable day yet for paddling, with a warm sun and a very slight breeze that seems to be following us, of all things.

Clothes have seemed unnecessary, and we paddle in the buff most of the day. As the afternoon wears on, we're startled by the sound of an aircraft engine at low altitude — the first we have heard in almost a week. The bush plane zooms low over our heads, the pilot apparently has done a double take, and banks around for another look. The smiling passengers are all waving and, not embarrassed in the least, we wave back.

Camp is pitched at the junction of the Kaluktavik River (east shore) and Noatak (north shore) after making close to forty miles.

~ ~ ~

More than at any other time in our lives, and perhaps because of the long period of solitude we've just experienced, we find ourselves immersed in a deep relationship with the wilderness through which we are traveling. The unbelievably distant horizons, the far mountain tops, the purity of the vision as we gaze in any direction of the compass.

With no permanent human presence meddling in their lives, we have come to know and interact with the inhabitants who call these arctic regions home. The marmots, foxes and caribou have shown us much more curiosity than fear. It is an experience that fills our hearts with wonder. Fresh bear tracks are abundant. Though we have yet to see one, we have no doubt that the bears are watching our downriver progress.

There is a feeling that the three of us share — one of being on the very top of the world, with all that is occurring elsewhere being of little significance. But already, we can feel a sense of loss creeping in, our final river days just over the horizon, making us wonder if we will ever return to this awesome land.

~ ~ ~

An 11am start is the best we can do again though we had hoped to be on the river earlier. At noon, a low-wing, single-engine plane goes over very high and heading north. We leave the Grand Canyon with no sign of a real rapid.

Along the way, a loon swims ahead of us, diving and surfacing only for a second or two, squawking more excitedly between dives when she sees us closer. Finally she flies off in disgust.

Cricket and a red fox check each other out. Apparently both curious and fearless, foxes would often come into camp, sniffing our equipment and looking us over.

A smooth beach of small fine gravel beckons to us to bathe and eat lunch. We've just stripped down when we're joined by a female red fox. More curious than any we've seen, she comes within a few feet of each of us, inspecting us and all of our gear several times before sauntering off down the shore. The sun is warm and the rock collecting is good — all told, we relax for two hours.

The all-day, south-facing exposure to the sun has begun to take its toll on our skin. We apply plenty of sunscreen lotion and cover-up with hats and clothing whenever possible today.

Noatak Canyon welcomes us late in the afternoon, and we're delighted to find several good Class II rapids. It's such a beautiful place that we decide to stop early (7pm) and camp here, pitching our tent by a singing creek and climbing the hills behind us to watch the river and sunset. Just before we leave, two Inuits in a longboat with outboard motor pass by heading up river — probably hunting caribou. For the first time, stars can be seen at night (two of them!), since we are in the canyon.

The canyon is so beautiful, we can't help lingering a little longer than we had planned. Just as we are loading the boats, a bush plane flies low over our site and dips its wings. A brief afternoon rain shower and windstorm appear, complete with rainbow. We pass the junction of the Kelly River in late afternoon, where a U.S. Geological Survey team has an encampment of large white tents.

Just below the Kelly, several Inuit families have set up a hunting and fishing camp. Here we enter the huge maze of islands that is characteristic of the river all the way to its mouth, where it empties into the Arctic Ocean.

We look at possible campsites, one with the tracks of a mother bear and two cubs, but finally choose another that has several sets of very large tracks. David finds a gnarly circular root (a dead one) in which we build a fire that burns all evening. He still has enough energy to try his luck at fishing.

The night is slightly dimmer, but still holding light on through 'til morning. The quarter moon is bright — for the first time — just before setting beyond Asik Mountain. David pulls in a beautiful five-pound char at midnight. Two meteors flare briefly in the southwest sky.

~ ~ ~

As usual, we sleep well into the morning. The nocturnal fishing efforts have pushed departure back a bit more and we're off at noon. After the human activity yesterday above the Kelly River we feel as if we're really back in the wilds again.

Then, late in the afternoon, we meet a party of eight Germans in six boats, four of them Metzelers like ours. They started at the Cutler River seven days ago, so have been about a day ahead of us for the past week, until today. They must have paralleled us for a while through one set of island channels, then joined our route at the tip of a large island. They'll finish at the village of Noatak where a plane will meet them.

We play tag with the group for three hours through the islands, burning up the miles in the process. Finally, the Germans take the right side of an island and we take the left. Twenty minutes later, we find that we have come out a quarter mile downriver from Noatak. We can see the village, but have islands and a heavy current between it and us.

Noatak Village does not beckon to us in any case — it's evening, and we don't have the desire to do or buy anything there. More than that, we have built up a sense of solitude that has become the core of our trip — a bonding among the three of us as well as with the wild and beautiful country through which we're passing.

Perhaps two miles below the village of Noatak, the river is bordered by ice cliffs that continue for another quarter of a mile. The current has cut into the tundra in a wide curve, eroding soil and banks as high as 25 feet, exposing solid ice in the permafrost layer.

Chunks of turf and mud keep falling into the river as we paddle past. A cold wind blows from the ice and the whole thing has a medicinal smell — like a billion Band-Aids, as Cricket points out. Every once in a while we pass a tree whose leaves have turned golden, reminding us that it's already half-past August, nearly a quarter 'til fall.

Rapidly eroding mud banks have exposed an impressive layer of permafrost as David paddles in for a closer examination of the band of ice.

Paddling another five miles or so, we make camp on the downstream tip of a pleasant island. The two stars are visible again, even though we're not in the canyon. Nights are just slightly dimmer. David fishes and friendly tongues of flame warm us at our campfire.

As we drift off to sleep, two feelings flit in and out of our consciousness — the sadness of being in the last days of our journey and the uncertainty of the ocean crossing that lies ahead of us. But having passed the village, we're now committed to the crossing.

~ ~ ~

We wake to a warm sun on the tent and are on the water by 10:55am, soon passing an Inuit family that has set up a fishing camp. When asked, they reply that the fishing is good, so it must be *really* good!

The sound of an outboard motor behind us grabs our attention and soon a longboat with three persons aboard comes into view. We recognize the crew from Kotzebue as they ease their boat close beside us. Sweetie-pies and oranges are a welcome treat and we give them some beef jerky in return.

Cricket and Dave are really pissed, and let me know it, in no uncertain terms, as I make a command decision to turn down the offer of a ride in the longboat back to Kotzebue. I feel that, years from now, my kids will look back on this trip and be proud that they paddled every mile of the river themselves. Our friends assure us that our boats will do fine on the ocean crossing, and they will look for us in Kotzebue tomorrow night.

As we leave the maze of islands, the river widens and deepens and the current drops to almost nothing. We pick up a crosswind and every mile is hard-fought. From the Nauyoaruk bend to the mouth of Lower Noatak Canyon is physical agony. Every time one of my kids catches my eye, I can feel the angry darts that come flying my way over the declined offer of a ride.

We're so exhausted that we stop and dig into the main food bag for more beef jerky. Though we had hoped to cover a greater distance, we stop at 9pm and camp on the south shore at the entrance to Lower Noatak Canyon. We briefly enjoy the beautiful sunset, but clouds are moving in quickly — the temperature is dropping — tomorrow may not bring favorable weather for the ocean crossing.

~ ~ ~

Wow! We're packed and underway by 10am! We head into the canyon, which is beautiful country, but the paddling from here out is pure, tough work — no current to help out. A light rain falls sporadically, then in the afternoon the sun breaks through and the day grudgingly clears.

Each leg of the river — and there are only four of them left today — is a major one, taking hours to paddle. The river is so wide, it is difficult to gage our progress — it's likely two to three miles between the riverbanks in this area. We've packed double lunches and extra jerky, for we know this will be our longest paddling day yet.

Backs ache, arms ache, butts ache. We've been churning against the wind for eleven hours, the last hour and a half alongside Kinuk Island, the final piece of the Noatak Delta. The temptation to stop and camp is overwhelming.

At 10pm, we slide past the downstream tip of Kinuk with only a huge question mark ahead of us. Ten miles of open ocean. Black night. Exhausted bodies. Are we being smart or stupid to leave all land behind and commit to crossing at this late hour?

A farewell sunset lights our progress on Kotzebue Sound, as we finish our last and most exhausting day of paddling.

A spectacular sunset — like embers of fire stretched across the sky — has been underway to our right for almost an hour. The lights of Kotzebue twinkle on the horizon, barely visible. But the ocean is like a mirror — not a breath of wind stirs. No matter how we feel, we know that this is the time to go.

A mile out, an Inuit family slows their outboard beside us and a young man offers a ride. We decline. Though our aching muscles might disagree, the three of us are now into making the total trip under our own paddle power.

Halfway across the sound, we polish off the last of the jerky and gorp. All around us is silence, except for the muted dip of our paddles in the water. The western sky is now blood red behind the mountains and on the watery horizon. Seals break the surface of the color-drenched sea to pause and look at us, turning their heads from one side to the other. As we twist around and make eye contact, they slide quickly out of sight.

I watch the sweep of black water behind Cricket's and Dave's kayaks and know that we must still be moving forward. At last the color fades and the wakes become invisible in the night. Cricket sings to help take our minds off the physical exhaustion — John Denver, Jim Croce, Simon and Garfunkel, Barbra Streisand.

It's dark now, except for the knife-edge sliver of light at the horizon — impossible to see each other, even a couple of boat lengths away. But Cricket's singing is the beacon that holds our exhausted trio together — without it we will lose each other in the darkness.

A layer of cloud and mist hugs the water, gradually winking out the stars above and moving ever nearer to us from the open ocean to the west. If it catches us, our bearings will be gone, we will try to find each other, hold on and wait out the night.

The lights of Kotzebue gleam closer and we begin to make out the shapes of low buildings behind the glow. It's midnight, we've been paddling close to 14 hours, but now the end is within our grasp. At 12:15am, we slide quietly out of the darkness and nudge the shore at the foot of Mission Street. No wave laps the beach — the ocean is still a black sheet of obsidian.

But Kotzebue is alive and hopping. An old man weaves his way down the street and staggers toward home. Teenagers walk arm in arm and Honda motorcycles raise dust clouds on the gravel street. The noise and smell of gasoline engines seem strange to our senses.

It's been hours and hours since our last pee stop and now it's a screaming priority! Dave and I step behind a fishing boat while Cricket scurries around the corner of the nearest building. Privacy is the last thing on our minds.

Relieved, I head toward the construction trailer a quarter of a mile away, where the crew is just climbing into their sacks. A friendly greeting, and they pull on their boots again, pile into the truck and head for the water. Boats, gear and people are whisked aboard in moments and we're back at the trailer for hot soup and hot showers. We somehow manage to chat a bit, then curl up on the floor for dreamless sleep at 2:30am.

We're awakened at 7am by the crew piling out for breakfast. The morning is a shuffle of gear from river bags to airline bags and washing of clothes in between. We're able to book space for the three of us on Great Northern Air for an afternoon flight.

Then it's a last-minute scramble to clean, dry and pack the boats. While I'm dismantling them, one of the Inuits working on the apartment building comments on our trip and I recognize him as the man who offered us a ride as we were starting our crossing last night.

Before leaving Kotzebue, we again run into the longboat crew who had made the crossing a day and a half ahead of us. They had run through four and five-foot seas the whole way, taking on a good bit of water, even in the big boat. With conditions like that, and depending where the wind was, we could have taken six or eight hours for the crossing rather than two. We definitely went at the right moment!

Many years have now passed since that early morning when, exhausted, we pulled our kayaks from the water on Kotzebue's shores. As we re-entered our familiar, modern world that long-ago August, we had questions even then. What would the trip mean in times to come? Would it fade from memory and lose significance as other rivers swirled through our lives?

It's now safe to say that our time on the Noatak was perhaps the purest wilderness experience of our lives. I know that a yearning for those uncomplicated days on top of the world still burns brightly within my heart, nearly forty years later, and the three of us often talk of that trip as we gaze upriver once more.

~ ~ ~

Following the Noatak adventure, the Alaskan Lands Act, which returned territory to Inuit, Tlingit and other native tribes, as well as setting aside irreplaceable wilderness and wildlife areas, was a hot national issue. Having firsthand knowledge of these lands, and a heart connection to them, Cricket, David and I wrote letters, visited senators and representatives, and even testified at a national hearing in Atlanta. Our voices, as well as countless others, helped protect large areas of wilderness in Alaska.

A Wilder Place

Our southern Appalachian classroom, as close as our front door, was ideal for homeschooling in a natural setting. It would seem that nothing could pull us away from this unusual, but satisfying, living experience. Yet something did.

Trish, a native of Washington state, had, for several years been encouraging — as part of our children's education — a living experience in the West, while the kids were still young enough to benefit from it. We discussed several areas that we had seen in our western travels that we thought might be good possibilities.

Trish favored the tiny community of Stehekin, nestled in Washington's North Cascades. Surrounded and isolated by National Park, remote peaks and forbidding glaciers, it would be hard to imagine a more ideal setting for being in contact with the natural world. However, knowing the cost to rent a summer cabin there, I felt that it would be far beyond our means.

When I said that we could never afford a Stehekin rental, Trish immediately took it as a challenge and was optimistic that it wouldn't be a problem. Within the month, she stepped off the *Lady of the Lake* at the Stehekin landing, set up her tent at Purple Point, and rented a bicycle. Within four hours, after knocking on doors in the tiny community, she had found three affordable rentals.

Trish called me from the boat landing, the location of Stehekin's only phone. We compared and discussed what she had seen, chose together, and three months later the whole family was heading to Stehekin for the months of October and November.

Stehekin promised — and delivered — another deeper layer of wilderness for those two months in 1998. The isolation is akin to what you would expect to feel in rural Alaska. There are no grocery stores. Food and other supplies come in by boat or barge from the east end of 55-mile long Lake Chelan. No roads connect Stehekin to the outside world. Most folks arrive on the *Lady*, a four-hour journey uplake. Backpacking in from the north, or coming by float plane, are also options. Snow blankets the community from November to April, often reaching a mid-winter depth of five feet. About eighty hardy individuals call Stehekin home year-round.

The *Lady of the Lake* plies her way between Chelan and Stehekin, a four-hour journey made once a day, except in winter when the schedule is more limited.

On the first day of October, we walk down the gangway from the *Lady of the Lake* into our new world, taking in the red of vine maple, the yellow of cottonwood and the dark green of fir and pine, snowy peaks rising beyond the forest. At the boat landing, Wally Winkle has parked his vintage Ford pickup, keys in the ignition, for us to use. We load our packs into the back of the truck and while I drive, the rest of the family hops onto bikes for the seven-mile up-valley ride to our new home, an inviting two-story A-frame.

The kids and I split and stack large rounds of fir that Wally already has on hand for firewood. The living arrangement is small, but warm and cozy as we enjoy reading, both out loud to the family, and to ourselves around the woodstove. Trish and I have a bedroom for two while each of the kids has a bunk in the loft.

No matter which trail you choose, the North Cascades will take your breath away. The visible lake is Lyman, where we were camped; Upper Lyman, beyond the tree line, is still frozen over.

We enjoy several mellow weeks of October weather, hiking the Rainbow Loop, Agnes Gorge and getting to know virtually everyone in the community. The boys, ages 12, 9 and 5, decide they want to give the one-room K-8 school a try, Schoolmaster Ron Scutt is agreeable, and our crew increases the school enrollment from eight to eleven! Autumn, at 15, is "too old" to attend the school and so continues to study at home.

One of our two months has already passed. Then the unexpected happens. It is as if Trish and I have the same seed taking root in each of our minds. "The kids are happy and our time here will end in a few weeks. Do you think we could stay on through

Christmas, maybe even to the end of the school year?" We have a family meeting to discuss the possibility. There is agreement. Enthusiasm!

But we aren't by any means sure that we can pull it off. Wally's place is already committed to other renters after we are scheduled to depart and there are few places in the valley that can accommodate a family of six. A chance encounter with Babe and Berneita Miles, as they are leaving the valley for the winter, reveals that their house could handle our family, and just may be available indefinitely. We jump at the opportunity.

But there are two more necessities — a four-wheel-drive vehicle that can handle the winter, and a larger wood stove that can heat the whole house since our family will be using all of the second-floor space. As we guess, neither are available in Stehekin, nor is the Internet, so I take the Lady downlake, book a room at the Parkway Motel, and search the "for sale" ads of the Chelan, Wenatchee and Spokane papers.

It seems a fruitless search, and I am ready to catch the *Lady of the Lake* uplake Friday morning (there being no Tuesday or Thursday boats in the winter), when out of the Thursday morning papers, both items that I want suddenly appear as new listings. There is a twelve-year-old 4WD pickup with a camper shell in Entiat at a price we can afford and a large airtight woodstove in Spokane that will be perfect for our space.

I call both numbers, reach only the truck owner, and immediately drive the 45 minutes to Entiat in the van in which we had come west. We make a deal and he agrees to deliver the truck to the barge dock in Chelan. I call the Spokane number again without success, but leave a message, "Don't sell that stove, I'm on my way," and start the three-hour drive to Spokane.

Both the truck and the stove just make it onto the barge for one of the last uplake trips that winter. By now the snow has descended into the valley and the kids and I are scrambling hard to cut and split the six cords of firewood needed to see us through the winter. We have been warned to move quickly, even with four-wheel-drive, both with getting the firewood in and transferring our belongings to the Miles' house. November is sending snowstorms to the valley every other day and if a heavy snowfall descends while the truck is at the house, it will be there until the spring thaw.

Canyon, at age 7, muscling a sledfull of supplies to the house. Rivers, age 11, heading to the one-room school on a snowy February morning.

Again, we make it, but just barely. The truck is parked under a large fir tree out at the valley road where it can be shoveled clear in order to access the six-mile route to the landing, which is plowed all winter. We can meet the boat with our truck to pick up the grocery order, then bring it back to our snowed-in road where we will pull it in by sled the third of a mile to the house.

Snowshoes are a necessity for making that trek, which crosses one of the river channels on a small bridge and gives you a feeling of deep solitude as you pass through the dense green wall of snow-covered cedars. With the short days of winter, there will be weeks when the boys and I, getting ready for the journey to school, will buckle on our snowshoes in complete darkness, sometimes watched by a sliver of new moon above McGregor Mountain. Our winter coats always contain two small flashlights, so that we won't miss the trail, even if the first flashlight fails.

And snow it does, that winter of '98 – '99. Twenty-nine feet fall between November and April, often reaching a depth of six feet on the ground. Snow sliding from our roof piles up to completely cover our windows, requiring regular shoveling. And, each time we bring in firewood, we silently thank the neighbors who had advised us to build a snow tunnel for access to the wood-shed.

Rivers and Forest sledding off the workshop roof.

Winter evenings find us relaxed in the main room, the woodstove warming us through, reading an exciting book out loud, or perhaps reading to ourselves, or working on writing a school paper about the October cider-pressing, or the annual spawning run of the Konkani salmon in the Stehekin River.

There comes a knock at the snow-sheltered door, accompanied by the clatter of snowshoes or skis being removed. "Hey there!

Just thought we'd come over and see how you're doing," as neighbors Ana Maria and Laurie shake the snow from their parkas and gladly accept our offer of a cup of hot tea.

As with every member of this small community, these two, though petite, are deceptively tough and resourceful. Ana Maria, one of the mainstays of trail maintenance in the North Cascades, once survived a skiing accident to drag herself for hours through deep snow until she could reach help, her companions having gone on ahead, unaware of her predicament. Laurie, with near-total responsibility for maintaining Stehekin's huge historic organic orchard, is an expert on pruning, irrigation and the necessary grunt work, along with ideas of how best to share the apple crop with the many bears fattening up for winter.

The winter isn't easy, with the demands of unexpected truck maintenance and plumbing repair, further complicated by working in the snow and sub-freezing temperatures. But we are still there — and smiling — when the sun finally begins to melt our well-packed snowshoe trails and pelt us with snow bombs from the fir branches yearning for springtime.

And with spring comes the melting, the glacial run-off and … the flooding. The meadow between our river channel and the valley road becomes an intimidating water barrier — with a current to give you pause. Once — and only once — we wade across, clinging to small trees, up to our waists in the icy water, all the feeling in our lower extremities having departed by the time we reach the valley road.

I string 400 feet of sturdy rope between end points and a few intermediate trees, then attach our river raft to this line with carabiners so that we will have a means of safely ferrying family, groceries and daypacks across the flood. The water persists for weeks and, of course, once part of the family goes out, the remaining members are house-bound until the first party returns.

By late May, the water has receded to normal river flow and we are able to drive to the house. Bicycles replace skis and snow-shoes. The whole community celebrates the Trillium Festival — one of the Stehekin rites of spring — with a potluck, music and games at the orchard. School morphs into summer.

The boys learn how to tie fishing flies from Tim, a local expert, and ply the waters of the upper valley for trout with barbless hooks, catching and releasing their quarry to the sparkling waters.

Though we have not lived here all of our lives, and lack the accumulated experience of the old-timers, we feel as if we have handled the challenges of winter in an acceptable fashion. We believe that we are now part of the community and once more we raise the question of staying longer — even, perhaps, permanently. We consider the future and look at the few private properties available for purchase within this vast national park.

The summer does nothing to deter our family's enthusiasm for Stehekin or the wild country surrounding it. Trish introduces after-school games, such as "capture-the-flag," in the late spring, games which all ages can enjoy. The warmer season is full of potluck meals, events in which the entire community participates. I alert our North Carolina renters that there is the possibility of our place there going up for sale.

~ ~ ~

Back in Stehekin, during our second winter, we travel downlake to drive south, camping and biking in the canyon country of Utah and Arizona. On the way back, just after crossing Blewett Pass, we are rear-ended at high speed by a Jeep Cherokee. The van is totaled, the bikes mashed like pancakes, and three of us are taken to the hospital in Wenatchee. The six of us were all wearing seat-belts, which undoubtedly prevented more serious injuries.

We recover, Autumn's neck injuries taking the longest time, but now have no downlake vehicle. A few weeks later, I fly back to North Carolina, check on our renters, perform maintenance on our house, road and pond, and see if our Isuzu Trooper is running well enough to make a cross-country trip.

Seven kayaks and canoes vie for space on the roof rack above and the interior of the Trooper is piled to the ceiling. I round up our four cats — with a bit of gourmet food trickery — for the journey west. Being outside cats, they have never before been confined. With a high-pitched chorus of feline complaints emanating from the two animal carriers, my radio turned up to double the normal volume, and a pounding thunderstorm trying to throw us off course, we nose west through the mountains of North Carolina and Tennessee.

The night before I leave, the home phone rings and I recognize the all-zero code of the emergency phone at the Stehekin boat landing. "I don't want to bother you," Trish says, "but I think maybe I should. The truck broke down yesterday and we've had no luck getting it to run or finding out what's wrong. I thought you might want to pick up some parts in Chelan."

"Uhhh, yeah, maybe..." as I run the possibilities through my mind. "Without knowing the problem, it could be quite a list of parts." More lost sleep.

Leaving our North Carolina mountain at 4am, napping in rest stops, and fighting gale-strength winds that threaten to lift the boats right off the rack, we struggle west. Three days and nearly 2800 miles later, the cats and I pull up at the barge dock in Chelan, where I unload the boats into the warehouse for a later trip uplake. With clean cages and the Trooper safely parked, the now-quiet cats and I board the *Lady of the Lake* for the trip home — at this point it is hard to distinguish whether home is in the East or the West.

Without the ability to receive a phone call or email, Trish will have to guess as to the day of my arrival — will I have a red-eye endurance drive to make the Wednesday boat or a couple of good nights' sleep to catch the *Lady* on Friday? Chances are, she will meet both, just to be certain — that is, if she can borrow someone else's rig. When the Wednesday boat noses into the Stehekin landing, she is standing at the dock, and I immediately hear her story.

Expecting to deal with the puzzle of a dead vehicle stranded in snow, I am astounded when she tells me that our rig has been returned to the head of our snow trail, apparently in perfect running order! Casual inquiries have turned up no leads as to the identity of the "masked midnight repair person" and it is only through a slip of the tongue the following week that the actual angels are revealed! It is a gift that we'll always cherish — it speaks of modesty, of caring and of the quality of life unique to Stehekin.

Her engines drone on in a soothing monotone as the *Lady of the Lake* plies her way northwest between snow-draped mountains, carrying a dozen passengers and winter supplies up-lake to Stehekin. We are quiet for most of the four-hour trip, our minds musing on what it might be like to live permanently in this spectacularly beautiful, but isolated, settlement.

Certainly not Utopia, but with a powerful tug on our hearts, this unusual community has captured us. We soon put our North Carolina home up for sale and begin to look seriously for property in Stehekin. This is problematic, we know, since less than 400 acres of private land exist within the vast North Cascades National Park and the few pieces we already know are available have exorbitant asking prices.

We keep turning over the same familiar stones. This piece of land has flooding problems. Another piece is half swamp and should be called "mosquito central." One seems much too close to its neighbors. And the owners of these — mostly absentee — will not budge on price.

Suddenly, out of the blue, comes news that a small cabin on high ground, with a view of 300-foot-high Rainbow Falls, is about to come on the market at an unbelievably fair price. We rush to the boat landing, call the real estate agent in Chelan on the emergency phone and tell her that we want to buy. Then comes the bombshell — even though the property has not yet been listed, another party has just signed a contract on it, only hours before our call.

The disappointment is huge, but we still have our rental place in Stehekin for as long as we want it. And our North Carolina home remains available to us. As time passes — and our original two months become four years — we begin to realize that, despite the richness of the Stehekin living experience, this tiny community is socially isolating for our teenagers. We hear the mountains of Appalachia calling us back.

Autumn will be starting her studies at Guilford College in Greensboro, North Carolina, the boys will have an opportunity to combine high school sports with their home schooling, and

Trish is poised for more direct action in social justice as our country teeters on the brink of another war in the Mid-East. Despite the sadness of leaving friends and pruning the roots we have put down in Stehekin, we look again toward the East with anticipation of a new chapter in our lives.

But before we pack up our current lives and send them downlake on the

Looking upriver from our Stehekin cabin.

barge, another opportunity knocks on our door. Literally a stone's throw from where we are renting, a small piece of land — less than an acre — is discretely offered to us at a reasonable price. We accept.

We return to North Carolina, but continue to rent — for one more year — the Stehekin home that we have so enjoyed through four winters. That last summer sees us in Stehekin once more, racing against time to build a small cabin that can give us a toehold in this rugged mountain community. Using lumber that I have helped a neighbor mill from old-growth fir and a generous quantity of discarded material (from the Park Service burn pile), my son Rivers and I create the largest building that Chelan County will accept without a building permit.

Our 8x15-ft Stehekin cabin, that we designed and built before the current popularity of tiny houses.

Our one-room "castle" is 8 feet by 15 feet, smaller than some people's bathrooms. And, of course, our Stehekin bathroom is a pit-type outhouse, our drinking water comes from the glacial flow of the river 80 feet away from our doorstep, and our bathtub — shared on occasion with visiting bears — is a deep spot in the icy river channel known as No-Name Creek.

We built on the highest spot on the property, so when the record-breaking flood came later that autumn (2003), it washed out our little bridge, buried a stack of boards destined for the cabin's interior under several feet of silt, but left the cabin itself untouched. My oldest daughter, Cricket, came up from Oregon the next spring and together we dug out, cleaned and installed the interior wall boards.

A concerned bear wonders what we're doing in his bathtub — the deep spot in No-name Creek.

The cabin was livable — even before the work that Cricket and I did — and I spent the month of April trudging through the melting snow, crossing the swirling No-Name Creek on a cotton-wood log, and using the solitude to finish my first book, appropriately named *Wherever Waters Flow*.

Now the cabin is a family destination for some combination of us every summer, the kids bringing friends to challenge the icy waters of the lake, backpack the many trails of the North Cascades, and connect once more with schoolmaster Ron Scutt and old classmates from the log-cabin schoolhouse that might reappear.

The isolation of Stehekin is of a sort that you don't expect to see in the U.S. south of Alaska, and in this age of creature comfort and consumerism in the United States, something that few could tolerate beyond a brief summer vacation. Yet, despite the comparative ease of living on our North Carolina mountain, we all realize that the experience of Stehekin was a rare gift, one that will call us back time and again.

Canyon (left) and Rivers (right) enjoy an icy dip with friends in Lake Chelan.

Lives We Had Never Imagined
Waking Up To Guatemala

Why did we select Guatemala as an immersion experience for our family? Certainly the surviving Mayan culture, embodied in both the Mayans of today and their artifacts that have survived the centuries were factors. But we felt there was much to learn about this country and its people, facts that were difficult to sort out in our own country. With a large measure of both surprise and sadness, we found that we were correct in that thinking.

With Autumn 17, Forest 14, Rivers 12 and Canyon 8 in February of 2001, our time with the Guatemalan people would provide a new dimension to our learning experiences.

~ ~ ~

There came a restless spirit to our family in the winter of 2001. Deep snow covered the tunnel to the woodshed, our snowshoe trail to the valley road was well-tramped, and we had read book after book beside the warmth of the woodstove. The mail came and went only three days a week, as the boat delivering it plied a similar schedule.

It was our third winter in Stehekin, Washington, and we felt that we had finally learned how to roll with the punches of an environment over which we had little control, to enjoy the many periods of solitude, and to appreciate the small, vital community of which we were now a part. Autumn pursued her own brand of self-directed learning and the boys embraced the creative projects at the log schoolhouse.

But once again, the time had come to change gears and move our classroom into the unknown — in this case, Guatemala. As with all of our travel, there would be no formal lessons, no textbooks carried with us, simply open minds, open hearts — and open journals. We would stay as close to the people and the land as we could, which wasn't difficult with our dirt-bag style of travel.

We carefully planned and packed — clothing for a radically different climate, some basic food items to get us started, a photo book of our life at home, small gifts (mini-flashlights and personally made notecards), light-weight sleeping bags (even though we knew that we'd be staying with families in their homes, or in hostels part of the time.)

Leaving Stehekin in winter always requires a list of logistics before even thinking about the ultimate destination — shutting down water and draining pipes, getting gear and yourselves through the snow to the boat landing six miles away, making sure of space on the boat with its limited schedule, assuring that your downlake rig is ready to roll, checking to see if Blewett and Snowqualmie Passes are open to traffic, and making sure you have a place to stay the night before you fly.

~ ~ ~

All checked off and we think we're in the clear. Not so fast! As we leave Blewett Pass behind and head for the Interstate, we begin to hear reports of a massive 6.8 earthquake in the Seattle-Tacoma area — hundreds injured, billions of dollars in damage, but miraculously, no one killed. We're soon detoured — the quake has caused a slide in the Maple Valley community, damming a creek, which has in turn flooded the route over Highway 18 that we had planned to take.

As we wind our way closer, more reports come in — the airport control tower has been trashed, a temporary control center set up in a field, and only about 30% of Seattle's flights are operating. Motels are overrun, our original reservation doesn't work, and we end up grabbing a marginal room as a last chance.

Our previously booked 12:30pm flight through Miami is listed as "delayed" (it hasn't even arrived yet) until 1:30, 4:30, 6:30 and finally they're talking about the next morning. While I call our Miami motel to cancel, Trish goes into action, elbowing her way to the counters of other airlines, and amazingly comes up with a routing (Alaska/American/Lacsa) for our family of six that will work, flying through San Jose and Los Angeles, arriving in Guatemala City at seven in the morning. This is not the first time she's pulled a trip-saving airline change out of the hat!

On our midnight flight out of Los Angeles, our seats are scattered all over the plane; I'm wedged between two large strangers who probably wish I weren't there as much as I wish they weren't. Sleep, always difficult for me on an airplane, is impossible tonight. Carrying only daypacks — no checked luggage — for our upcoming month has allowed us to be much more flexible,

able to quickly grab a different flight, when the opportunity arises. And we make it — we're actually on a flight headed for Guatemala!

It's a sunny, seventy-degree morning when we finally touch down in Guatemala City. The airport is not crowded, we change a few dollars into quetzals and catch a taxi to the Casa San Jose. The folks there welcome us, even at 9:30am, make up our beds

Autumn's watercolor of the Casa San Jose's entry hall.

and let us nap the day away. We pick up bread and fruit at a local market, but the cheese, tomatoes, powdered milk, cereal, crackers and peanut butter that we've brought with us from home come in very handy. Autumn paints a beautiful watercolor of the interior hall of the Casa San Jose.

Breakfast is hearty and welcome — porridge (somewhere between tapioca and oatmeal), scrambled eggs, black beans and tortillas. We find a taxi and are off for the airport, where Autumn tracks down an email service. Messages are sent to family back East and friends in Stehekin, letting them know that we arrived safely, despite the Seattle earthquake.

Our plan is to head directly up to Tikal, to see for ourselves the magnificent stone temples that were the heart of the Mayan Empire centuries ago. Our Taca flight to Flores is in a low-flying, twelve-passenger, single-engine plane that lets us have an intimate view of the jungle that we'll soon be exploring.

~ ~ ~

We catch a mini-bus to the village of El Remate and soon settle into open rooms at El Mirador Hostel — a laid-back place with great vegetarian food, as it turns out. Air temperature in the nineties and high humidity are a shock, just having left the snows of Stehekin. A swim in Lago Peten Itza helps refresh us.

The El Mirador is an unusual place — from our standpoint, at least — with many arches, windows and undefined openings in the whitewashed adobe walls, with a basic foundation of bamboo covered with local soil. Stairways tend to be steep, with irregular steps. They'll keep your climbing legs in shape, but beware of the sudden drops.

All rooms — bedrooms, kitchen and dining area — are open to the hall or patio — not a door in sight. The baños and showers have curtains. There is a cave for keeping packs in relative safety, with very steep steps descending into the ground. Each night, a man stretches out across the top of the steps as a guard against theft.

~ ~ ~

In the morning, a cacophony of wild jungle noises greets us — birds, animals and insects, augmented by the many roosters of the village. Pigs, horses and dogs wander everywhere. No TVs or gas stations interrupt the natural sounds.

We hang out around the village, buy some vegetables and fruit, and stay close to the hostel, hoping to hook up with Jeff, Josette and Raven, best friends from Washington's Lake Chelan, who are expected to join us here. No luck today.

Although we hear tales of robbery and worse, we make arrangements for going to Tikal tomorrow. The veggie dinner at El Mirador is delicious — soup, rice and squash. Canyon enjoys playing with Shanti, the blond daughter of Cat and Pepe, the only other folks from the U.S. that we've seen here. She is eight, the same age as Canyon, and hails from Humboldt County, CA.

~ ~ ~

We're up at 5am and notice that the village below is very much alive at this early hour. Women walk the main road with baskets balanced on their heads. Bicycles, so loaded with firewood that you can barely see the rider, weave along the margins of the road. Three little girls, chattering to each other, balance beautifully decorated water jugs (full) on their heads as they climb the steep road beside us. A bus, with brake shoes worn through to metal, does a long screeching stop on the opposite side of the road.

We prepare for the journey to Tikal, packing water, lunch, sunscreen and cameras, the cameras being the only items of value that we take. Robin, the mini-van driver, arrives promptly at 5:30am and we head north toward Tikal. Only in the last year or two was the road paved to help bring more tourists to this center of Mayan civilization, and to give a boost to the local economy, of course.

Making our way, with half a dozen others, along the winding path toward Temple IV in the dim pre-dawn light, we have fleeting feelings of what it must have been like to live here a thousand years ago. The day will be hot, but as the first light filters into the jungle we're thankful for our jackets. Howler monkeys swing through the branches while a multitude of different birds call beneath the canopy. At Trish's suggestion, Anne Marie, a German woman traveling alone, has joined our family for safety. Our footsteps take us past stellas and small stone structures, and after perhaps a twenty-minute walk, we reach the temple.

We all climb the many steps up the steep, unexcavated sides of the temple, finally arriving at a narrow open terrace ringing the upper structure. Ascending another group of wide stone steps, we reach the top just as the sun rises over the jungle.

The temples in the plaza are visible above the misty green canopy as we move in their direction. Our kids, and Canyon in particular, enjoy exploring the many rooms and passages in the acropolis and other buildings surrounding the temples of the plaza. Canyon discovers tiny foxes hiding behind one wall, and we all see coatimundis (even a family of little ones) scooting here and there.

Temples I and II, facing each other across the plaza, are impressive, and most of us make the long steep climb to the top, even though at least two people have been killed in falls from the open steps.

Later, back at the El Mirador, a tarantula confidently makes its way across the floor of the dining area. Jeff, Josette and Raven have arrived. We swim together and share our trip impressions, making plans for the morning.

~ ~ ~

At dawn, we rendezvous with our friends, catching a mini-van to the rarely visited ruins at Yaxja. Deep in jungle, one side each of a couple of temples has been cleared of soil and vegetation, giving the visitor a glimpse of the majesty that existed a few hundred years ago. Most of the stone structures in the temple complex are now ghostly shapes and mere suggestions of the vibrant communities that once existed here. How quickly the earth will reclaim our human attempts at permanence.

The exploration is fun for both our climbing muscles and our imagination. We sleep soundly, despite knowing that tomorrow will take us into new territory and experiences, as we head toward the Mountain School near the Mexican border.

~ ~ ~

We're packed and ready, with an early morning van ride to Flores, then the quick flight in the small single-engine Cessna back to Guatemala City and thence by bus to Quetzeltenango (Xela). We search through filthy streets on foot for a hotel room that might fit our budget, finally choosing the Hotel Quetzalteco, with its hot, stuffy closet-sized rooms and outside toilet. It would be more

Buses being loaded in Guatemala City. Though the retired U.S. school buses might be 40 years old, each bus is brilliantly and distinctively painted so that it can be easily identified and matched with its destination by those in the know.

refreshing to be camping, but that's not an option tonight, and tomorrow we'll be on the road again.

We head down to the Minerva Terminal (one of several "bus yards") — where, we've been told, we'll find the bus to Colomba. To picture such a place in your mind — think of perhaps fifty retired U.S. school buses, average age thirty years, scattered about in no particular order.

Wandering bus to bus, we enquire of the destination of each, and are finally directed to a wildly painted one that we hope is the one we want. The roof of the bus is being loaded. A few pieces of luggage go up, but mainly baskets of fruit and vegetables, a young pig, a pair of goats and the requisite cage of flapping chickens, which give meaning to the commonly used term, chicken bus. Two "assistants" will also ride on the roof to make sure nothing is lost, and that the animals behave themselves.

Keeping our packs on our laps, we slide onto a couple of vacant, well-burnished bench seats. We know that if we don't occupy them three to a seat, we are sure to get squeezed by a new arrival at the next stop. Fellow passengers scrutinize us from head to toe, as we are the only "Yankees" on the bus. We smile and try a few words in Spanish, usually eliciting a grin and a chuckle, and a reply that sails over our heads.

We aren't going to Colomba, even though the bus is. We are told that the tiny village we're headed for can be reached down an unmarked dirt road that intersects the paved strip that we're on, several hours out of Quetzeltenango. The bus driver says he knows where we want to get off, but just to be sure we ask several other passengers until we find one who assures us that he will tell us when we come to the spot.

A pretty, pony-tailed girl of about three stands close to stare into our eyes, not an iota of self-consciousness in her face. Loudly chewing, the gum suddenly flies out of her mouth and rolls through the filthy grit of the bus aisle. She dives down, retrieves it and pops it back into her mouth!

The road winds torturously through the heavily vegetated mountains, the bus straining to stay on the narrow pavement. Suddenly there's a cry from seemingly all the passengers on the bus, a host of pointing arms, and the bus brakes to a stop. It takes us several minutes to squeeze our way to the exit, but at last the six of us are standing at the roadside as the bus disappears around the next bend.

Not a person nor a building is in sight, only a narrow dirt road that descends steeply into the jungle, looking as if it might be impassable in rainy weather. Are we really at Nuevo San Jose and Escuela de la Montana (The Mountain School)? Well, we need to find out quickly, since few hours of daylight remain.

As it turns out, the walk to the tiny village is much shorter than we imagined it to be, and we're soon introduced to the school, the learning area, and the bunk beds where we'll sleep. The village has sporadic electricity (a few hours a day) in the school office and no telephone service — no communication of any sort.

Meals will be taken individually, each of us with our own Mayan family. Even Canyon, at age eight, will make his way through the village alone to eat with his host family at mealtime. The families serve us only what they would normally eat, this often being a single boiled egg or baked potato, plus a bit of broth. This immersion is expected to improve our Spanish through conversation with family members, though many of the older folks speak only the Mam dialect of the Mayan language.

Local instructors meet with us for two to three hours each morning. I have always been slow to acquire new language skills, though Trish, and particularly the kids, rapidly absorb all that is offered. But language is not the only benefit of this experience.

A group of young women and men from several countries are working with children and young adults in the region under a program called "Play for Peace." It's our first contact with the group, an international organization promoting friendship with others across the lines of cultural, religious and political boundaries.

Their goals and activities mesh so completely with our own family's view of reaching out and embracing others that we quickly become friends, sharing ideas and personal histories. They are also housed at the Escuela de la Montana, delighting the children of the village with games, face paint and T-shirt design projects.

Three days after our arrival, we are invited to accompany the PFP group to a neighboring finca, a coffee plantation, to share enthusiasm with the children of workers who live there. We travel most of two hours — even though the finca is not that far away — down a torturous dirt road, standing in the back of a pickup truck. A firm grip on some part of the truck, or at least a fellow "standee" is necessary for survival.

A dozen of us pile out of the truck as it grinds to a halt, but not a child is in sight. We are told that most of the children here have never seen a visitor, let alone one with a different skin color. Moving to an open area, the PFP folks start batting a beach ball back and forth among the group. It's obvious from our laughter that something involving fun must be happening!

Unable to resist finding out what we're up to, a small face emerges from a leafy hiding place. Then another. A "come join us" gesture, coupled with a big smile is resisted at first, then hesitant steps bring a boy of about seven or eight close to us. As he bats the beach ball, others come out of hiding, including colorfully dressed little girls with their hair carefully brushed and set in pigtails.

Soon the group of kids outnumbers us, and Trish forms the younger ones into a circle for a game of "duck-duck-goose," only this time it will be "gato-gato-perro" (cat-cat-dog). The older children can't resist joining in, and soon the circle has grown. At some point, Trish and I wander away from the games and the stares of the kids who have never seen folks wearing a white skin, to peek into some of the other parts of the finca.

We're introduced — with our very limited Español — to Ximena, a gray-haired woman of perhaps seventy. We understand enough to realize that she holds a place of honor in the community, and graciously accept the invitation to see her room. Her twin bed with iron frame and a flat webbing of springs appears to have come straight from a college dorm. It stands on a concrete floor, a rarity in this village of earthen floors. A single framed photo-graph hangs on one wall while the others are bare. But the photo itself, black & white, and somewhat faded, shows the Guatemalan National Football (Soccer) Team, year not indicated. Ximena proudly points out a handsome young man, her son, in the photo.

Unable to resist a fun time with new friends, shy children join a game of gato-gato-perro on the coffee bean sorting floor.

Trish and I sit on the thin bed mattress while Ximena pulls a rare treasure from the clutter of a cardboard box in the corner — a 12-ounce bottle of Coca-Cola. Before we can refuse (neither of us normally drink carbonated beverages), she has twisted off the cap and thrust it into my hands, a beaming smile on her face. Realizing that this is her ultimate gesture of hospitality, we share the Coke among the three of us and express our genuine appreciation.

~ ~ ~

Back at the Mountain School, the lessons continue, Spanish often playing a relatively minor role compared to recent history. We realize, perhaps subconsciously, that our days as tourists in Tikal have passed and that we're rapidly becoming students — all of us.

It is here that we meet Aurora, learning of her personal involvement and heartbreak in the decades-long civil war. The role that the U.S. played in the conflict as they trained the Guatemalan military to intimidate and murder their own people, wiping out entire villages so that U.S. fruit corporations could take over prime agricultural land. She was a commander in the resistance, with the daunting task of handling logistics for a large group of guerilla soldiers, a group with the ability to fade into the countryside and become invisible when faced with the insurmountable numbers and superior weaponry secretly supplied by the United States.

Aurora, an attractive woman in her early forties, sits with us and a dozen other students in a circle, her long dark hair framing a serious face that has seen more than its share of tragedy. With flashing brown eyes and animated gestures, she tells us through a translator of her experiences in Guatemala's unbearably long, just-ended, civil war.

How she was able to procure and distribute supplies while remaining undetected, yet give birth to and raise two children through the turmoil, and escape into Mexico in the most dangerous times. Of the reasons why they fought, trying to keep their land — despite the attempts of foreign fruit corporations, with the aid of Guatemalan troops, to wrest it from them. Of seeing her brother and uncle executed before her eyes at a government check-point.

So much loss — sorrow that we have difficulty imagining. Soldiers trained to terrorize and kill their own people if they show any signs of standing up to foreign money interests by mentioning human rights or — God forbid — organizing a union. We read. We researched. We were appalled.

~ ~ ~

Rivers and a friend collaborate on an art project in the more relaxed evening time at the Mountain School.

Our days at the Mountain School pass far too quickly as friendships with our individual families deepen. Those who must leave during daylight hours work at one of the fincas scattered throughout the mountains, earning the equivalent of a dollar a day for their labors in growing, harvesting and grading coffee beans. Younger and older family members spend their day with the never-ending chores of survival, often trekking miles to collect just a single bundle of firewood for the cooking fires.

Many generations live under the same roof. The elders are respected and cared for by their descendents in a manner nearly forgotten in our own country. Nursing homes for the elderly are an unknown concept for Guatemalans. Likewise, the word "mortgage" has no counterpart in their language. You build your home with what you have on hand, in as short a time frame as possible, with the help of the whole community.

The name of this village, Nuevo San Jose, gives a clue to its sad history. There are a number of Mayan villages that bear the prefix "Nuevo" to their name, indicating that there was once another of the same name. They date back to a time of terror and blood that stretched over decades, when village after village was exterminated in the name of "fighting communism," the inhabitants never having heard the word, let alone the philosophy. Survivors, usually few, banded together with the remnants of other villages to try to resurrect their lives following the 1996 peace accords.

A powerful poem written by Autumn tells of the anguish of those terrible times, as the village of Dos Erres ceased to exist one bloody morning.

Desaparecido[6]

Bare rocks and pitted earth hold
     scarred trees   touching jagged sky
as gently as the streams that run like warm tears
over the face of the land.
     You will find me here
    Between shadows and red flowers.

Walk with me
among the rivulets of birdsong
gray fog brushed by quetzal wing,

    among these stones and fallen limbs.

Tierra Quemada.
that is what they called it.
Los soldados, our countrymen...silencio
      I ask you hear
Come,
I know that it is not easy,
            ...they swarmed out of those trees over there
take hold of my hand
ghosts will not hurt you.
Por favor
touch the earth,   *...spirits trained out of them*
hear among the whispering weeds.

See the way the sunlight, trickling like rain
touches the heart of this red flower
and glows
      in the soil over my shattered bones
It is the color of the shirt I was wearing
            Tierra quemada.
         trained in a school on US soil, paid
            by taxes of your people,
Small and threadbare, the shirt
not as bright as my blood.
      I was only five.

I ask you hear the wails   *in stillness*

because you know loss
but only your own.
I, touching raw earth,
know them all.

They were here to fight communism,
            So you were told,
Come,
sit with me on this hillside
where the jungle green has begun to heal
            and the sky still weeps.
I died here with my village
Mi padre, my baby sister, everyone
I had ever known.
I wore my favorite red shirt.

            ...you say you will never forget
        but what of the horrors   never half remembered?

It was early morning,
tortillas cooking   dogs barking
old women hauling firewood.
        Sunlight spilling through doorways
my mother was singing.

Los soldados,
they swarmed from those trees
        and the morning air cracked suddenly
splintered with machine gun fire
            ...but trained in counter-insurgency warfare
they killed us instead
children running, screaming
"mama, mama, nos están matando!"
        "Mommy, mommy, they are killing us!"
Anguish, swept away by death.
Desaparecido en la sombra.

Dawn light traces dragonflies
and cielo.
I ask you here
to stand
with the clarity of sunlight on water,
among the shadows,   and the weeds.
That your tears
mingling with sunlight and birdsong
flowing over this scorched soil
may nourish the red flowers
springing rain-touched from the earth.

The massacre at Dos Erres occurred in 1982 and, although more than 200 men, women and children were tortured and murdered in the most brutal fashion imaginable, the tragedy there was only one of 226 documented massacres throughout Guatemala in the 1980s. At the site of Don Erres, the evidence (bodies, many of whom were still alive and screaming) was thrown into a dry well and buried. Over thirty years later, it is said that no grass or other vegetation grows on that site.

~ ~ ~

The history that we were learning was intense, and called for a period of evaluation and reflection. We headed for Lago Atitlan by bus, over twisting mountain roads, the driver taking every opportunity to pass, despite the absence of safe passing zones. Autumn had just remarked that she had seen nearly every scary driving scenario, when our driver pulled out, with very limited visibility, to pass a tractor trailer. Immediately, an oncoming

6Spanish words in the poem: *desaparecido*: disappeared; *sombra*: shadow, shade; *cielo*: sky; *soldado*: soldier; *tierra quemada*: scorched earth, referring to the Scorched Earth campaign of terror and genocide in Guatemala — the majority of soldiers who carried it out trained at the School of Americas at Fort Benning, Georgia.

tractor trailer roared around the blind curve, causing us all to offer a final prayer or curse, depending on our personal philosophy. Both truck rigs moved their outer wheels onto the non-existent shoulders while our bus somehow slithered between them without even losing a mirror!

After bringing our racing hearts under control in Panajachel, we look for a luancha (small boat) that will take us across 5100-foot high Lago Atitlan to the village of San Marcos. For a total of $10, the six of us are ferried to our destination across this fabulously beautiful lake, once a volcanic caldron, surrounded by mysterious peaks.

San Marcos gives us a welcome, but selfish, break from the intensity of the history which we are learning — a history necessary for understanding the harsh, and often tragic, lives of those whom we've come to know as friends. They have no opportunity for such a pause in their own daily routines.

The village is quiet, and as we walk uphill from the lake, we pass several tiny shops from which emanate delicious food fragrances, as well as a market with appealing fruits and veggies that appear as if they've just been picked. We find a hostel with thatched roof huts, a secluded feeling, and space enough for our family. Trish stretches out for a welcome nap.

Our several days pass quickly in this small village as we enjoy the food and explore the shore of the lake, finding an awesome spot on the rocks to dive and swim. Autumn connects with Aumrak, a Mayan shamaness, and spends time each day with her, studying intuitive healing. Forest and Rivers team up with a trio of Irish students to take on five local youths in a boisterous soccer match. The game is played on concrete, where falls are bruising and bloody but, unbelievably, the visitors manage to edge the locals by a goal.

All too soon, we must gather our drying clothes from the branches of bushes close to our hostel, stuff them into our packs, and arrange for a luancha to meet us at the small lakeside dock. The chicken-bus trip to Quetzeltenango is relatively uneventful, and soon we're meeting the city-dwelling family with whom we'll stay.

We visit the roof, where we can hang our wet clothes on a wire to dry and make the acquaintance of the resident roof-dog. Virtually all city dwellings have a vocal dog who guards the roof from intruders entering from that direction. This means, of course, that you can rest secure, but on the other hand, may not be able to rest at all amid the canine chorus.

At the language school, we each find the instructor with whom we'll be matched for our time in the city. The instructors are skilled, but we miss the close family atmosphere of the Mountain School. The school library, however, is extensive — including many volumes published in English — and we are soon delving into more Guatemalan history, a history difficult to find back home.

U.S. support of the Guatemalan military was kept secret during the Reagan Administration, and it was not until the 1990s that the documentation showing U.S. involvement was declassified and made public. This triggered a United Nations-backed truth commission investigation and an official apology to the Guatemalan people by President Clinton in 1999. This is not meant to absolve any political party in the U.S. for what has occurred in Guatemala. Corporate greed and our own apathy have been the culprits. And it continues today.

That the intimidation tactics used by the Guatemalan military in over 90% of the human-rights abuses were taught at the School of Americas became well-known. Fort Benning, Georgia — where the school (now known as the Western Hemispheric Institute for Security Cooperation) is located — became a lightning rod for protest against the teaching of terror tactics to the military of South and Central American countries.

When we returned home to Washington, and a year later to North Carolina, we continued to educate ourselves on the abuses — intimidation, murders and disappearances of union organizers and human rights workers — occurring in neighboring countries to the south and linked to SOA training. What we learned fanned the flames of social justice for us, and soon we were part of the activist group at the gates of Fort Benning each November.

~ ~ ~

Once again, but with a fresh outlook, we return to Guatemala City before boarding a flight home. The street people reach our hearts much more easily than when we first arrived — the old man without legs, the lady who can barely drag herself from the curb onto the grass, the blind ones. Victims of the long conflict? We empty our pockets of quetzals, our hearts wondering which atrocities or tragic turns in their lives have brought them to this moment.

What will this time mean to us all when we return to our own country with its fixation on consumption? Two words come to mind. Awareness. Compassion. Perhaps in the small ways of our own lives, we will be bridge-builders rather than wall-builders.

Could Anyone Do This?

"Sure, adventure traveling sounds like a great way for a family to go, but we could never do it — it's too far outside of our comfort zone," you say. "Our family isn't like yours... We don't have all those outdoor skills... Our job only lets me be free two weeks a year... We don't know how to find safe places to stay, or how to handle our money in a different country... How do we deal with a medical emergency? We don't know the language... You know how to do all these things... We'd be stuck..."

Ah, so it seems. But do you really think we knew how to deal with every situation before we set foot out of the U.S. or into a wilderness area with kids in tow? Not by a long shot. It was a learning experience for us as parents as well as for our children. The secret is in taking small steps — enjoying situations that stretch you a little bit, but where the rewards are obvious before you head out.

The single most important factor in moving into family adventure travel is the desire to do it. You can find a hundred reasons to delay or not to walk out through the door at all.

When our daughter, Autumn, was born, Trish and I knew how to ride bicycles but had never ventured into the realm of bike touring, let alone doing it with a wee one. But we thought it could be a cool way for the family to be more intimately involved in travel experiences.

We discussed the possibilities. We researched gear. We sought out the knowledge of an experienced bike-tour leader at a nearby outfitter. Not only did he share his wealth of knowledge with us, but invited us to join him on a week-long ride in northern Florida.

We came away from that trip with enthusiasm and a desire for the next one. And Brett, the trip leader, became a life-long friend with whom we've shared many more adventures.

So, how should you start? Your own background of experience and your family comfort level will determine that. If you are short on wilderness skills, perhaps the first trip should be close to home. Maybe in your own yard, if the outdoors is new to you and you have a good spot for a tent. If there is a safe and appropriate place for a campfire, so much the better. Your little one(s) will be entranced by the flames and embers, will learn how to build and feed the fire, and will be absolutely delighted to cook mouth-watering biscuits wrapped around a stick.

Is there a state or national park near you? Chances are, there will be a convenient one. You can easily move the family camping experience to the next stage, taking with you the skills that your kids are learning, but adding the discipline of having to prepare and think ahead, so that vital pieces of equipment or supplies are

Children love to be a real part of outdoor adventures, taking responsibility for meaningful chores. Autumn, at age 7, finishes erecting one of our two tents on a family bicycle-camping trip.

not forgotten. Make lists. They, of course, will be modified every time you go out, but will be invaluable as each trip takes shape.

As these experiences become familiar to the family, think about the adventure toward which you are working. Is it backpacking? Bicycle touring? A river or lake trip? Each of these will require different equipment, but all will have one characteristic in common — your gear will be lighter and more compact than it was for family car-camping. I'm not saying that you have to go out and spend a fortune on high-end, ultra-light equipment, but on the other hand, you'll soon get tired of lugging around a 15-pound family tent on your back.

Heading for the trail? Weight will be a larger concern here than on bicycles or in canoes. If you have a child under two years of age, chances are that you will be toting her in one of the many child packs available today. These have additional compartments where you can stow diapers, snacks, extra clothing, raingear and other small items needed by the child. This will leave your partner with the balance of the camping gear, including tent, sleeping bags and pads, food, cooking gear and more, which makes for a pretty hefty load.

However, as the infant becomes a toddler, more is possible and may even be demanded by the wee one. A small day pack or fanny pack containing snacks and a rain jacket, or even the family lunch, carried by that beginning hiker can go a long way toward a feeling of contributing to the group.

Our son Forest, a determined hiker at two years of age, made the entire trek into Shining Rock Wilderness — four trail miles and 1200 feet of elevation gain — on his own two feet. We directed his attention toward brilliant leaves, shiny acorns and their caps, and holes at the base of trees that could be possible animal homes. We made up stories that went with them, so that the trek became an intriguing adventure rather than just a long hike.

Autumn had a small wooden arrow that I had carved, about three inches long, on a leather thong around her neck. Her "hiking award." For each hike that she completed, a notch was added to the arrow.

Sure, when young ones are this age, you're probably relatively young and in decent shape yourself. Nevertheless, you want this to be an experience that discourages neither the child nor the parents. Consider two factors that can help make those first trips more user-friendly.

First, limit your early backpacking to short treks, no more than two or three miles, particularly if you are in mountain country. Second, consider a "no-cook" menu, where you can eliminate stove, fuel, and most pots, making packs lighter. However, keep in mind that a beautiful destination and tasty food enhance the total experience.

~ ~ ~

How will a bicycle touring experience differ from a backpacking adventure? First of all, your back and shoulders will feel a bit of relief — though your legs will not — as the infant/toddler rides behind you and traveling gear is carried in panniers or fastened with bungee cords behind the child seat. Remember that your little ones will doze off while you are pedaling, and if they are in a child seat their heads should have additional support such as an Ensolite pad folded to extend above the seat back. If you are pulling the child/children in a detachable trailer, it will have additional storage space, as well as providing protection for the kids during rainy weather.

Unless you are an extremely hard-core biker and gravitate toward trail riding, your bicycle touring experience will not be in wilderness. You will need to take into account the road characteristics and conditions along your route. How busy is the traffic? Is the route better at certain times of day? Does it have bike lanes? Are the shoulders narrow, wide or do they contain annoyingly placed rumble strips.

The road distance you can cover bicycling is, of course, much greater than your trail range as a backpacker. However, you will still need to plan ahead. Where are the campgrounds on your route? Do you need reservations? Are there hiker/biker sites which give preferential treatment to those traveling on foot or by bike? If you are staying in cabins or motels, be sure to reserve them before you start. Where are the grocery stores along the way which allow you to resupply?

Again, a short overnight bike outing in your home area will serve as a shakedown trip if you are not yet familiar with bicycle touring. Have you forgotten a critical item? Are the kids happy and enthusiastic? If not, why? How is your own attitude? Are you sharing with the kids the vision of the trip — what you're seeing along the way, what you're looking forward to around the evening campfire? Are they getting enough breaks and snacks? Do they need another favorite book or stuffed animal with them? Ask them. Make notes for next time.

~ ~ ~

And then, of course, there is the paddling trip, be it on a lake or on a river. Having your gear in waterproof containers is necessary not just for the weather, but for paddle splashes and the unlikely event of a capsize. An appropriate PFD (personal flotation device) is mandatory, of course. This means a head-supporting collar and crotch straps for infants. A swimming pool or pond test with the little one should be made before setting out, in order to test the effectiveness of the PFD.

As you try a lake for the first outing, pay particular attention to the weather forecast, avoiding high winds and long distances on open water. Make sure that the shoreline has suitable places for camping. If you have chosen a river, be certain that any whitewater is matched to your paddling ability and that the water level of the river is considered not too high to be hazardous, or too low to be navigable.

With all of the many types of outdoor adventure, the comfort and happiness of the child is primary. If you are to do it again and again — to make it your family way of life — you must have the support and enthusiasm of your smallest adventurers.

~ ~ ~

Whether you're experienced travelers, thinking you're out of options because you have children, or a family that's new to and entranced by the thought of adventure travel with kids, take a look at the Appendix of this book for practical ways to move your family in new directions.

Yes, we all still enjoy family adventures as adults! Here, the gang relaxes at the end of a week on the Grande Ronde River in Oregon in June of 2014. L to R: Forest, Doug, Trish, Rivers, Ty (Autumn's guy), Pete (Cricket's guy), Canyon, Dave, Autumn. Front: Cricket holding Jessie Jane.

Who Are We Now?

When a child is nurtured, loved and supported on her journey into adulthood, comfortable in any environment, from navigating a remote wild river in Nepal to adapting to multi-generational life in a Mayan village in Guatemala, or simply exploring the mountains in her backyard, you might question the results.

But it should be clear by now that it has never been our intent to push any of our children into specific careers, least of all those involving power or disproportionate income. From an early stage in the children's lives, they were exposed to our basic philosophy, which embraces the value in, and story of, every individual with whom we come in contact. The understanding that we are here to observe, to learn and to put into practice the lessons that appear every day.

That we are not here to simply make our lives more comfortable. That material wealth is not a worthy goal in itself. That there are those whose lives are at the very margin of existence because of our own daily actions and consumptive habits. These are lessons that we, as parents, must continue to be conscious of in our own lives each day.

Understanding such a philosophy, reinforced with personal experience, is the gift we have tried to give each child. From that point on, the choice is theirs. Of course, we also hoped that they would learn the value of living simply, awareness of the needs of others, and an intimate knowledge of our natural environment, eventually weaving these together with meaningful vocations that give a glow to their hearts.

Each of the six has now grown into adulthood, with wild country in her or his blood. Each adventure has helped shape the person who lived it. What has been the effect of wilderness? Of non-traditional schooling? Of getting to know individuals in different cultures? In the words which follow, I've included each person's own voice, which speaks to some of these questions.

A family grown. Rear: Doug, Trish, Rivers, Canyon, Forest, and Autumn. Front: Dave and Cricket. On Thunder Creek.

Autumn

Mountain Girl

Born at the full of the moon,
*   By mountains you've been kissed.*
Like floating islands they rise
*   In a luminous sea of mist*
Bidding a welcome to...the mountain girl.

Born at the autumnal equinox
*   From whence you took your name,*
A sense of balance and fairness
*   Now and always the same*
Go with...the mountain girl.

Your talents abound,
*   Your purpose seems clear*
With love in your heart,
*   There's nothing you fear*
For you are...the mountain girl.

Already you've crossed the seas
*   And climbed the mountain side.*
But turning your eyes toward home
*   You watch the heron glide*
For you'll always be...the mountain girl.

Now it's hand over hand
*   As you reach for the height.*
Sometimes it seems dark
*   As doubts cloud your sight*
And you wonder, am I still...the mountain girl?

But how can we tell you
*   Who've been there before,*
The storms are your strength
*   And you're entering the door*
To becoming...the mountain woman.

— Dad for Autumn on her 11th birthday, September 1994

Our daughter, Autumn, has long been a leader and inspiration to the rest of the family when it comes to independence and self-reliance. Her many skills are enhanced by her talent as a writer, and her environmental and social activism more than once have caused a politician to slow down or change course.

Today, when Autumn speaks out at a hearing on issues close to her heart, she is often mistaken for a lawyer. "Wow, she left those commissioners no room to wiggle," is a frequent comment from others in a controversial county meeting. Autumn learned, early on, how to thoroughly prepare to address an issue, and how to use words to accomplish change. At the tender age of 14, she was chosen by Macon County to fill an adult seat on the Solid Waste Advisory Committee as the County moved into the age of active recycling.

Autumn's own words follow, giving the reader a glimpse of her feelings toward the natural world, new friendships and travel.

~ ~ ~

We are grinding up a huge hill above the sea, Dad and I. Dad's legs straining and his T-shirt soaked in sweat, bike pedals slowly circling, and me snug in my sturdy plastic child carrier behind him. I'm free to watch the pancake rocks, yet convinced I am part of the effort, at least so far as a hill ration of Cadbury fruit and nut chocolate bar is concerned. When we pause to refuel, Dad breaks off the little waffle milk chocolate pieces, with the rumpled dark raisins sticking out the sides, and hands them back to me. Seabirds swirl around the huge sea stacks, which really do look like towering piles of pancakes, delighting me. The ocean crashes in sheets of white spray far below.

My earliest childhood memory is of loons playing with me. I was nestled in the center of a canoe between Mom and Dad, their own tiny baby bird. The black and white loons bobbed up and down, and I, delighted by the game, bobbed up and down with them. I'd peep over the canoe's gunwale, and then hide below it. We were on the Bowron Lakes in British Columbia, Canada. To this day I have a feeling of beautiful connection with them, and the experience of being deeply regarded and embraced, included by other creatures.

When I think of something that defines my parents' approach to life and to our education, it is a thrilling tickle of curiosity. My folks fed me. Boy, did they ever. They fed my ravenous mind, my bubbling creative impulses, my fascination with texture, my hunger for connection with different ways of thinking and peculiar sorts of people who lived mysterious lives. Somehow they knew that they didn't have to push me towards knowledge or teach me how to learn, they just had to pour fuel towards the spark of learning. In nonlinear ways.

Pour they did. My mom, a brilliant and gifted teacher, believes that language development and vocabulary are based on a child's participation in an incredibly broad range of experiences. Words picked me to play with them when I was pretty small. Sometimes a poem would come tumbling out at the swingset, with urgency, and I'd pop over to Dad whom I knew was always handy with scraps of paper and a pen in his leather glasses case in his shirt pocket. He'd be ready to lovingly write a dictation as I blurted out a verse, so that the sweet little winged thing didn't just fly over the ridge without me. Mom made beautiful books for me out of large pieces of manilla paper and string, and would take lengthy dictations about sheep and castles and witches, which I'd illustrate. Later, she encouraged mad, inventive spelling neatly scrawled across pages. She didn't allow spelling itself to get in the way of what it existed to support. This listening, discovering and finding followed in our travels, and gave me the basis for composition in my life. Based in improvisation, I rely on an ability to follow wild inner nudges to unknown ends.

I remember my fascination with sinkholes in New Zealand. It was clear to me that they could suck a farmer right down through his field as they had the very old Moa birds, and they had that queer bright green color around them. I remember crossing a high swinging bridge near a waterfall, carrying my fairy box — a cardboard egg carton to which I carefully added magical objects from nature. On a sandbar, Mom and I picked up scallop shells bigger than my palms that had lush, bright colors. I remember noticing that there were other people moving about the islands like us, in beautifully crafted wooden caravans built onto trucks. Curiosity, for three months, led us in divine paths over the rugged landscapes — and I know that even at the age of 5, who I am was being fed by that trip.

Our family met the tall man who was like the BFG on that trip, in his long dark cloak, the man Dad calls a "person of mystery," a description I love. You could just imagine his doing things such as blowing dreams into people's windows with a trumpet, like the Big Friendly Giant in Roald Dahl's book. I remember that he took the time to bend over and relate to me. The BFG taught me to notice a small plant with a leaf like a long arrowhead (sheep sorrel), which I thought he called yarrow because that name came with me. Months later in my Mom's garden in North Carolina, I excitedly showed her the same plant growing in the pathways. I knew that you could eat it and enjoy its sour taste.

My experience of lands and travel was richly woven with stories and ballads as I grew. I remember Dad singing me to sleep for a nap to my favorite long ballad, Barbry Allen, a tragic love song, in a sweet room papered with rosebud wallpaper on a spring morning on the farm where we got to ride the red four-wheeler to herd sheep and the postman brought our groceries in brown paper sacks with a grin. Did people really die from broken hearts, I wanted to know. Dad figured sometimes they did.

Tales such as The Lord of the Rings and those of Merlin, King Arthur and Wise Child wove themselves into my relation to landscape and adventure in ways that are difficult to describe, but I know that stories are like provisions that help us on our way. One *of my life goals is to learn to tell a ripping good tale to children.*

Children have such expansive intelligence. It gives them joy when someone is genuinely interested in them, takes time to share with them, and especially knows how to sing a good song or tell a good story. Small children may seem to not yet have the words or vocabulary, but they may be experiencing the world as a spiritual and timeless whole in a way that, even as adults, we may not be able to describe with breadth.

My parents' travels with me were an essential gift to the growth of my soul, in ways that I particularly draw from in this period of my life. They also gave me the huge gift of time, unrushed, to choose what I wanted to do all through my childhood. To meander and dream. You don't always have to go through all the laborious steps to learn. By processing multiple layers through curiosity and random exploration, much can come to light. When it matters, you remember, and try applying it to new situations. Original thought can naturally develop and explode. Children's time should not be wasted by over-programming it for them. Their time matters even when they are small.

I feel there is a jarring tendency in modern parenting to fill kids' days with wholesome and edifying activities that are calculated to give the child an optimal advantage. Yet, in fact their time is so full, they have no chance to absorb the experience, and time becomes smaller because of being saturated with movement and goal-driven items. Comparatively, when a child can unfold in nature or in creative expression with no adult expectations, time can expand and layers of richness that aren't even apparent at the moment can be unleashed. There is something of trust in this. It's okay for things to be hidden, rather than exposed and asked for proof.

Well, perhaps one day our paths will cross and I'll get back to you on this and you can let me know what you've experienced. I just know that time, like children, responds to how it is approached.

When boxed into schedules, it contracts, yearning to burst out, and when freed, it responds in the most magical dimensions imaginable.

The concept of time can vary in different places and cultures. When I worked In Ireland, there was always time for a cup of tea. That cup of tea might last two hours, and there would still be time to get the work along in the fields, to feel the luminous light like lemon juice through the clouds, to laugh and experience a day well met. That's what drives me mad about the current speed of our lives, and the shallowness that being fragmented gives us. It is hard to experience a day well met. It never feels as if enough is done. But when you are experiencing unrushed time with no expectations on it — which is more and more rare — there is space for digesting your own life and the lives of others, along with time for the necessary tasks. Travel has let me experience aspects of space and time that are currently the central exploration and fascination of my life.

…Excuse me I've got to get a cup of tea…

Please don't think I've mastered this. I've postponed my deadline on writing this piece for my Dad for weeks, holding up publication of the book at the last moment, because of the wild rush of my life and frenetic days. But I'm crazily curious about the mystery of time, longing for a curvy experience of it, where I stop scraping my knees on the hard squares of my digital calendar that turn my time into blocks.

I love experiencing my life as part of a family. Over my chair as I write is a bright pillowcase painted with flowers that my brothers Canyon and Forest brought to me from the Pacific Islands, where they met activists at the heart of the movement around climate change and saw in me a poet mother of the Islands.

In my garden, garlic is pushing up green and saucy, which my brother Rivers planted in the fall, eager for a piece of soil as travel and medical school keep him on the move. It reminds me of his gift for laughter. Rolled on my desk is an amazing map of old Ireland, made for me and burned on the edges by my husband, Tiyo, who knows my love of roaming and of that island. Soon to be on my wall is an incredible print of fiddles and mountains by my sister Cricket, who knows about my heart. In my kitchen is a green candle from my brother David, to remind me of my light, and in my fiddle case a horsehair bow that he gave me. My aunt Libby's spinning wheel sits next to me, and I wear my favorite "confidence shirt" from my aunt Suzie, the smile of my uncle Jim from the mantel encouraging me to write. There's a photo of the lilacs my uncle Doug went up a ladder to pick for my wedding bouquet. I share my uncle Mike's green thumb and love of growing things, and aspire to my aunt Elizabeth's skill with sending loving cards. My uncle John's sense of humor which makes Dad crack up I also aim for, and my aunt Ginny's sweetness. My aunt Linda and I share a love for collecting beautiful things from nature, and shiny bits like ravens. I play a mean hand of Blackjack like my great-uncle Jack, so guard your pocket change. And I grow marigolds for him. Music boxes make me think of my grandfather Virgil. Already I've been writing of huge gifts of the heart my mom and dad have given me. Dad is a strong and gifted poet, who encourages me always. Mom loves my wholeness, and knows how to listen to my heart and give me hope.

This may be a little boring for you to read, and it's okay if you skipped some, but I tell you about it, dear reader, because I realized that the unity of time and space I feel at certain times is often warmly woven with the intimacy of family, or of community in places I have laughed and worked and drunk steaming cups with a company of friends in Ireland or Costa Rica.

I'm ecstatic to be married to a man who, when I wake up one morning and read an email from friends in the Netherlands, wakes up and says, "Yes, let's go to Bhutan." I could hardly believe it. I was only half-entertaining the idea, although I was crazy to go to Bhutan, and Tiyo was all for it. Together, we ate *amadatsi (cheese and chili) cooked over the fire in our camp of young people deep in the mountains, and drank cup after cup of British tea, Bhutanese milk tea and Vietnamese green tea poured by friends from those countries. Oh, delicious. We'll be on a new adventure soon.*

The openheartedness that travel yields, the ability to be at home in company, to befriend children ... ah, that is something that gives me hope for the world, and for the brightness of my life to come. My parents made bold choices to branch out from what was supposed to give results, and meet life on their own terms. Pathways that this opened in my heart and in my way of trotting around in the world are the deepest of gifts. Thank you, Mom and Dad. Thank you, sweet family. Thank you, beloved Tiyo, who adventures the world with me now and sees my spirit in its wildness. To time, with the heart of tea steeping until it is just right, toasting love.

~ ~ ~

Music has been an important part of Autumn's life from a very young age. She started playing fiddle in the Suzuki method, but always yearned to make Scotch-Irish music the primary part of her repertoire. It was not long before she found Lois Duncan, a mountain legend in these parts for her skill with stringed instruments. The two played Appalachian songs on the fiddle together for most of a decade until Lois' death in 2002.

Watercolor painting, as well as other mediums, spoke to Autumn's heart from a young age, and while in her early teens she created a series of wildflower prints, followed by a similar series of wild birds. Both flowers and birds were indigenous to the North Cascades and were sold as notecards in the Stehekin Craft Shop.

Following her graduation from Guilford College, with highest honors in Conflict Resolution and Peace Studies, Autumn spent a year in San Jose, Costa Rica, acquiring a master's degree in Environmental Security at the University for Peace.

Autumn embraces Bri-Bri friends in the remote Costa Rican village of Yorkin. Her master's thesis documented and encouraged the environmental work of the women living there.

Yorkin, a small Costa Rican village reachable only by dugout canoe, was devastated by a huge and sudden flood in 2008. Working to rebuild and restore Yorkin, she endured almost unimaginable tragedy in the loss of Benson Venegas Robinson, her working partner with whom her life had been so close. Benson's words about "success" live on, however, blending beautifully with the essence of our own family ethic: "Success is … your desire to be more, not to possess more."

Since that year, she has spent time in France, Ireland, and Bhutan, taught massage, and established the massage school curriculum at Haywood Community College in North Carolina. She is now building her own massage practice in Asheville. Bringing healing to others has always been a prime motivator for Autumn, and she has successfully developed several new bodywork approaches of her own.

A skilled writer and editor, including work with the Society of Friends, her poet's heart overflows with beautiful, sensitive thoughts and words. *Capital At Play* magazine, in their April 2016 issue, ran an eight-page feature titled "A Touching Practice," about her pediatric massage specialty.

Working in her home mountains of North Carolina, Autumn's path blended once again with that of an old friend from child-hood, and with a loving commitment to Ty Hallock, the pair were married in May of 2016.

Autumn and her brother Canyon, with good friends Rujuta and Vedashree, immerse themselves in the joy of the Ganesh Festival in Pune, India.

Forest

The Important Places

Child of mine, come
As you grow in youth
*   you will learn*
The secret places…
*   The cave behind the waterfall,*
*   The arms of the oak*
*   that hold you high,*
*   The stars so near*
*   on a desert ledge*
*   …the important places.*

And, as with age you choose
*   your own way*
Among the many faces
*   of a busy world*
May you always remember
*   the path that leads back*
*   …to the important places.*

— Dad for Forest, June 1986

When I wrote that birth poem for Forest back in '86, little did I know that it would come to life again 29 years later. Even less did I imagine that it would become an award-winning short film of the same name.

Forest, perhaps feeling that his dad was rusting in the joints a bit, or growing some moss on his whitewater paddles, invited me to run the Colorado River with him in the winter of 2013. I accepted, and at ages 77 and 27, the two of us piloted a 16-foot oar-raft for 28 days and 280 miles through the Grand Canyon.

Forest knew that I had made the same river trip in my homemade kayak in 1970; he had been studying my old slides and movies of that trip for several months, converting them to digital format. Here and there, when our paths converged, he would ask me about my early river-running days, filming me at the same time. If I questioned him about what his intent was, he would reply that it was historical information for American Rivers.

In certain respects, he was right. That was a huge understatement,

A still image from our Grand Canyon trip, used as the title image in the film, *The Important Places.*

however. American Rivers was supporting the project, along with @Gnarlybay and @Semirad, knowing that it could help combat threats to the integrity of the Grand Canyon. But the video was powerful beyond anything I could have imagined, and was as much a love offering to the child-parent relationship as it was a river story.

In April of 2015, Trish and I joined Forest at the Five Point Film Festival in Carbondale, Colorado for the premier. Only nine minutes in length, *The Important Places* was voted "most inspirational" and went viral on the Internet after its release. Emails arrived from friends that I had not heard from in decades, saying that they had been moved to tears while watching it.

Just yesterday, it seems, Forest was an eager beginner, shooting film, experimenting, and manipulating images in our home darkroom as an eleven-year-old. He went on to take courses at Rocky Mountain School of Photography in Missoula, Montana in his teens and returned several times to teach for the school during his adult years.

Now a sought-after freelance photographer, Forest has traveled to scores of countries, from Botswana and Norway to Peru and Australia. An accomplished rock and mountain climber as well as a skilled whitewater paddler, his photography and writing have appeared in a number of international publications such as *National Geographic* and *Outside* magazine.

He was Director of Photography for the powerful social justice documentary *Food Chains*, which recently debuted at the Tribeca Film Festival in New York City.

While still a student at UNC-Chapel Hill, Forest sold photos to stock companies such as Getty Images, which paid a significant portion of the cost of his last two college years. But through all of these experiences, he avoided being boxed in by conformity, keeping the light of creativity as his vision.

High on British Columbia's Claw Peak in the Waddington Range, Forest captured this shot of fellow climber Graham Zimmerman.

And to include Forest's own voice and feelings here, I've borrowed excerpts, with permission, from an interview that he did with Gary Parker for *Sea Stoke* magazine:

SSM: Tell us a little bit about where you grew up…

I grew up in the mountains of western North Carolina. My folks moved there from Atlanta, drawn by the mountains and rivers of the area. We grew up exploring by foot, bike and kayak. Our parents put an emphasis on experiential learning and encouraged us to spend a large amount of time outdoors, building forts in the woods around the house, catching crawfish in the steep creek that flows from a spring on the mountain, and learning to entertain and look after each other and ourselves.

SSM: When and how did you discover photography?

Some of my first memories of being aware of photography are from my very early years, perched on a stool in the basement of our house, helping dad rock the developer tray under the warm glow of the safelight in our small homemade darkroom. Seeing my interest, Dad gave me my first SLR camera, a Canon AE-1, when I was 10, and taught me how to expose, develop and print my own photos.

SSM: To me your images convey a beautiful sense of adventure, taking the viewer right into the location. You really throw yourself into your work it seems. How do you try to achieve this?

Well, I think it has been a trend in photography and advertising in the past decades to sensationalize and essentially "fake" a lot of imagery. It's somewhat ironic to me that things have gone this way because I believe it's much more difficult and logistically taxing to fake people having an adventure or being genuine and candidly exploring the world than it is just to grab a group of friends and go explore. I am lucky to have a great crew of talented and adventurous friends, and when we go on a trip there is nothing fake about it. It allows for a sort of genuineness and gritty honesty to come through that I think, when done right, have a timeless and relatable beauty. I take the photos that I want to remember, silly honest moments, moments of struggle and of beauty.

SSM: There is a growing disparity between the time people spend indoors wired to technology and the time they spend outside enjoying nature. Our relationship with nature, with ourselves, has broken down. Your photography is heavily focused on the natural world. What is your vision for the work you produce and how does it affect people who view it?

I agree that our relationship with the natural world, and the inherent knowledge of self that comes through exploring this world has, in many ways, been compromised by our constant connectivity to the virtual world. That said, wireless technology has also created an incredible platform for sharing the stories of those who are getting out there and exploring, and my hope in photographing and sharing these stories is that it inspires folks to go out and explore the world for themselves. If my work motivates a few folks to get up and walk around the block, talk to a stranger, climb a hill in the park or a mountain in Alaska and explore a deeper connection to this crazy world we live in, well then I am happy.

Forest exploring the climbing in Southern Spain.

SSM: Do you try to live a simple life? If so what are some of the things you try to practice?

Yes, I try. Some days I do better than others… Practicing gratitude is something that is important to me. I try to focus on being grateful for all that I have, in terms of material possessions, yes, but more importantly in terms of relationships, opportunities and experiences in this world. I think that it is in my nature to constantly want more, to experience more, to know more people,

to achieve more with my work. But it is equally imp
simplify and focus on all of the good things already in my ιιις, ς
to be present with the here and now.

SSM: What makes you happy?

Kind people, strange people, dark coffee, the magic hour, chance
encounters, big hugs, the smell of leather, surfing little waves,
climbing big mountains, the pull of a downstream current, long
open stretches of road, traveling to new places, returning to old
haunts, music turned up loud, the warmth in a glass of red wine,
the feeling of complete physical exhaustion after a day of hard
work or play, and the contagiousness of big laughs.

SSM: Do you have a favorite project that you have worked on?

I spent 28 days in November/December of 2013 on a rafting trip
with my dad and some other friends. Getting to spend that time
with my dad was so cool, and being disconnected from the wireless world for that long was really refreshing. Instead of Instagram,
each day I took 3–4 Polaroids and used them to create a big thick
journal from the trip. It was really gratifying to work with just the
film I brought, pen and paper and my hands to create something.

SSM: What about your plans for the future?

Keep exploring. Keep creating. Keep cultivating community. I've
been fortunate to travel extensively and to meet a lot of amazing
folks. For me the next step is not necessarily more travel, but
more time with those friends, peers, mentors and muses who
have been so important to my life and career in the past years.
My hope is to continue to focus on doing more with, learning
more from, and bringing together more of these wonderful folks.

Forest with new friends in Rio, Brazil.
"Raised by Woodwards and tamed by wolves, I am haunted by the allure of point breaks and powder days, steep creeks and tall peaks; I am a hunter-gatherer of natural light and candid moments. With an appetite whet with a taste of the unknown and the smell of home, I wander a path paved by open minds and trusting eyes, guided by willing feet ... and a desire to bring you with me." — Forest on forestwoodward.com

Rivers

Run Free, My Son

High on a windswept slope
   With crags and bristlecone stark
Stealing a kiss from the fleeting sun
   A snowfield sighs and then gives birth
To the rivulet hurrying down
   To nourish a harebell in its path
Tumbling on with urgency now
   Through fireweed, meadow and scree
Gathering strength and power soon
   To fill the canyon with song
Through the rainforest dark and deep
   Quickened by autumn storm
Oh river, your spirit runs free
   So always, my son, may yours.

— Dad for Rivers, January 1989

While still an undergraduate at the University of North Carolina-Chapel Hill, Rivers sent an intriguing challenge to the rest of his family one January.

"I want no birthday gifts from any of you this year. What I do want, however, is for each of you to do some specific personal service to better the life of someone less fortunate than yourself. This must not involve money and you don't need to tell me what you did."

Talk about a lesson in having our complacency turned upside down. What a gift *we* were given!

At the age of thirteen, Rivers may have received a gentle nudge toward his life's work. The two of us were in the woods on our mountain, trimming the branches from trees that we had taken down, when I made a mistake that allowed the chain saw to jump into the back of my leg, cutting it to the bone. Rivers dressed the wound, drove the truck to the house, phoned 911 for help, and then returned to wait with me for the EMT to arrive.

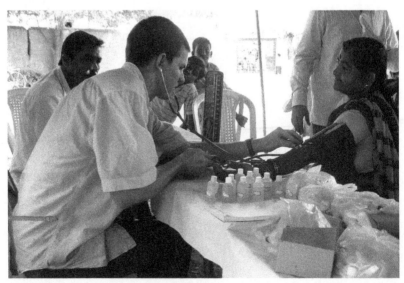

Rivers practices some of his Western medical skills as he learns traditional healing practices in Dr. Pengali's clinic in rural India.

As a coach for Special Olympics and a Big Brother to kids in need, Rivers embraced the clowning/healing style of Patch Adams, MD, and brought Patch to Chapel Hill for a weekend gathering of students, faculty and families, where Patch shared his lifelong philosophy of making compassion and love the primary focus of medical practice. Rivers also traveled with Patch to Haiti, helping in much-needed service work for the people of that country.

Ever the multi-tasker, Rivers created, and led, three new groups within his freshman medical school class. A handful or so of interested students would regularly come together in each of the groups through discussion and activities to gain greater appreciation of compassion in medicine, alternative healing concepts and wilderness medicine.

Having finished medical school and a MBA concurrently, and now looking toward his residency, Rivers encourages high school students in rural North Carolina, with hands-on projects and discussions, to pursue various fields of medical training through programs he has developed as part of his Albert Schweitzer Fellowship work.

His philosophy of reaching out to others, to know them as fellow human beings rather than simply "patients," is reflected so well in his personal statement for residency:

Soft clumps of coffee-colored soil yielded willingly to my bare hands as I dug a furrow into my garden plot. The rich scent of a recent rain on decaying leaves permeated my nostrils, and a deep calm came over me as I inhaled deeply. I placed each garlic clove with focused intention: orient upwards, press into the furrow, cover with loose soil, pat firmly, repeat. Methodically progressing along each row, my work took on a meditative quality and my distress began to fade. As I packed earth over each clove, it seemed hard to imagine that just an hour earlier the same hands, in a similar motion, had cracked the ribs of a middle-aged woman as we attempted CPR. I never knew her name or her story, but I was there when it ended violently. I believe that there is always something that we can offer patients, even if it is simply to sit and listen — yet this patient had nothing to say.

When I am caring for a patient at the end of life, I want to know her story. When her son flies in from Florida, I want to greet him as an old friend because I delivered him. I want to know what makes life worth living for her, and when that disappears, to provide appropriate care and calming presence to help her to navigate a peaceful final stage of life. I believe that rural family medicine will provide the space and community to facilitate such deep relationships with my patients.

Before college, I had never lived in a town with a population greater than three thousand. I learned to love the rhythm of life intertwined with nature and the collective spirit of tight-knit community. But I also saw firsthand the barriers to healthcare in remote areas. For my friend's father who died of a STEMI [heart attack] during a lengthy transport or for my elderly neighbor struggling to find a practice to accept her Medicare, health disparities abounded. Throughout my training, these initial glimpses have been amplified to illuminate the deeply ingrained inequality of health and healthcare that plague rural areas.

In my medical school class, I hardly needed a second hand to count the number of students with truly rural roots. And yet we know that this is the most predictive factor for a physician ultimately practicing in a small town. In response, a colleague and I started a two-county high school mentoring and internship program in Western North Carolina in order to lay the foundations for a rural healthcare pipeline program. Two years later our program has graduated 16 students, operates a budget of $15k, is being expanded to other surrounding counties, and is being integrated into a new state-funded rural training hub for medical education. During the same time, I served on the board of directors for the Western Carolina Medical Society and was involved in the effort to expand free specialty care for the uninsured to more rural counties. I am fighting for rural communities because *my patients are here, my parents live here, and my family will one day live here as well.*

It was not until my third year of medical school that I met my first burnt-out family physician. What terrified me was that she wasn't the only one. It seemed that everywhere I looked, there was another primary care doctor running on a treadmill, chasing RVUs [Real Value Units, a measure of effectiveness within the medical profession], with a speed setting out of her control. It was this experience and many like it that inspired me to pursue a MBA. I am convinced that, to practice medicine effectively, I cannot spend my life seeing 12 patients in a morning that have each waited weeks to receive an appointment. In business school I studied healthcare, operations, and entrepreneurship. I intend to one day create a clinic that I am eager to get to each morning and is accessible to my patients in a way that reduces cost to the system and improves access for those who need it most.

I am searching for a residency program that does not believe healthcare ends at the front door of the clinic, but rather supports residents to pursue innovative solutions throughout the community. I am seeking rigorous, broad-spectrum training that will allow me to be confident and competent when I am the only physician for miles. I am looking for a caring community that is collaborative, not competitive. If a co-resident experiences a difficult loss, I want to be there for a hug, a listening ear, or to help them plant garlic and find peace.

Fast-forward ten years from now. It is early afternoon on a beautiful spring day in southern Appalachia. I have just returned from four home visits in the far western part of the county and I am back early to see my first afternoon patient. He is struggling with depression and is having trouble articulating how he is feeling. I have 45 minutes with him and so I suggest that we take our visit outside for a walk in the clinic gardens. We pass a young boy and his mother who are planting long rows of sugar snap peas – they are part of our group visit program for children struggling with obesity. Our walk continues, and as we meander through rows of young plants, my patient begins to talk more freely. I find myself more present with him away from the EHR algorithms that are programmed to value only eight key questions in a visit for depression. I want to practice medicine in a place that allows me to be part of the community, to address the socioeconomic root of illnesses, and to always have time to sit and listen to my patients.

Always one to parley his opportunities into adventure, Rivers made the most of his two-week medical school break to see Norway and Sweden by bicycle, camping along the way. Here he pauses at the summit of a long climb in Norway, the road that he pedaled up visible in the background. Bottom left: Putting his dance moves to good use, Rivers douses his canoe jousting opponent; bottom right: Enjoying street revelry in Ecuador, February 2017.

Canyon

Canyons of the Spirit

There are...
    Canyons of the redwall,
    Thrusting above a fiery forest
       of autumn aspen,
    Kissed by a desert sea
       of sage,
    Spires wrapped in skies
       of indigo,
    Paths known only
       to the solitary hawk

There are...
    Canyons of granite and ice,
       rising stark
    From primeval moraine,
    Thundering rivers
       held in their grasp
    Still carving the land
       to nature's design.

There are...
    Canyons of the spirit,
       rich in ancient memory
       and wisdom,
       Filled with choices and paths.
Choose love,
    Not fear, my son
    and know them all.

— Dad for Canyon Sage, February 1993

Choosing a path that is uniquely your own can be very challenging when a string of capable siblings has preceded you. No one knows this better than Canyon, our youngest.

Having firsthand knowledge of the widespread struggle for clean water, as a result of our family travels to countries with a simpler lifestyle, he developed — in his early teens — a passion for making an impact on the problem. As a homeschooler, he organized and conducted four fundraising events — two 5K races that were very successful in helping to fund the water-quality work of Blue Planet in Central America, and two Empty Bowls projects, aiding the people of Haiti through Partners in Health as well as those in need locally, through Carenet. These projects made use of Canyon's skills as a runner and a potter, not to mention his knack for organizing and inspiring community involvement.

While friends were nailing their final high school courses in anticipation of favorable college responses, spring of 2011 found Canyon traveling on his own in rural Nicaragua, investigating and documenting the health problems of more than a dozen villages, problems linked directly to the lack of access to clean water. Often the village women and children — sometimes as young as six — would trudge several miles over difficult terrain each day, returning with jugs of tainted water, the only kind available to them.

After spending time in La Ceibita, a tiny village of seventeen families, Canyon relayed the poignant plea of one of the elders to us.

"I am old and already sick," said Margarita, "but I hope better for my grandchildren. I am glad to see how young you are; you give us hope for the next generation. I trust that you will spread the word. We need so much more. We'll be waiting for you here."

Powerful words, that Canyon did not forget.

All of this and more Canyon recorded with words and photos,

contacting the editor of our local paper directly from Nicaragua when he could find a point of Internet access. *The Macon News* responded enthusiastically, publishing the account of his findings in a feature spread over several pages.

As Canyon continued his research in Nicaragua, responses to his college applications began to arrive at home. With his approval, we opened each, and relayed the decision and financial aid award (if any) to him via email. Acceptances were nearly unanimous, but financial aid left much to be desired.

The University of North Carolina at Chapel Hill, a state school, was a financial bargain for North Carolina residents, and on top of that, they had offered Canyon a spot in the Honors Program. His brothers, Forest and Rivers, had already crushed it at Chapel Hill, graduating with dual majors, Phi Beta Kappa and Honors. In our minds — and we told him so — the decision was obvious. But to Canyon, the decision was not obvious at all.

He was not a follower and never would be.

Decision-time had passed, hope for a different outcome had faded, and a difficult college choice was made. Then, seemingly out of the blue, came a phone call from Harvard. A late acceptance, with nearly a full scholarship, was offered. This was the diverse academic atmosphere for which Canyon had yearned.

Once at college, Canyon's leadership emerged in several directions. In his freshman year, he handled the logistics for one of his professors with whom he helped organize a global water conference. Then, working with environmental activists Bill McKibben and Tim DeChristopher, and risking arrest on various occasions, Canyon directed his fervor into Divest Harvard, a movement to remove investment from the coal and oil industries.

The words which follow, a portion of the introduction to his senior thesis, speak from the heart and give a glimpse of Canyon's involvement and dedication to a sustainable-energy future:

The Harvard University Police Department lieutenant works his way towards us through a small crowd of about 30 student protesters. A University administrator and two officers follow close behind him. Six of us straighten up against the door of Massachusetts Hall, preparing for the possibility of arrest. We link arms tightly as the Lieutenant towers over us.

Supported by faculty and alumni, Canyon (2nd from right) and other activists blockade Harvard's administration building in an effort to establish constructive dialog with Harvard's president.

"This person needs to get in," he says, gesturing towards an administrator.

"Sorry, but we're blockading the building."

"Are you sure?"

"Yes. I'm sorry, but we're looking for an open and transparent dialogue with the Harvard Corporation about fossil fuel divestment, so we can only speak with someone who has the power to negotiate on behalf of the Corporation."

We hold firm as the lieutenant and officers pressure us to step aside. Finally, they turn around and walk away. James Claiborne, the chief deputy of operations, materializes and speaks with our police liaison at the outskirts of the crowd. It's early morning; university offices are just beginning to open. Donald Pfister, the interim dean of Harvard College, appears at the outskirts of the growing crowd, followed shortly by incoming Dean Khurana.

The dean of student life, Stephen Lassonde, informs us that if we do not move we will face disciplinary action from the administrative board of the university. The threat is chilling — academic probation or expulsion would profoundly alter our lives — but it is a risk we have steeled ourselves to face. We stay put, and reiterate our request to speak with somebody with the authority to grant an open meeting with the corporation.

Dean Lassonde melts back into the crowd. I find myself pondering how I ended up here, on the stoop of Massachusetts Hall. Raised in the beautiful backwoods of Appalachia, where political activity was mostly constrained to civil discourse over local issues, I was a stranger to protest of this kind. Attending Harvard on nearly full financial aid, I could never have imagined myself shutting down the office of the president and top administrators of the generous institution that made my education possible. And yet, I cannot in good conscience let Harvard continue with business as usual when that business consists of profiting from investments in the corporations that are driving the world towards catastrophic climate change.

My understanding of the climate crisis formed over the course of many years of education and experience. One of the most formative of these experiences occurred during a semester abroad when I was sixteen years old and lived with a family in rural northern India during their barley harvest season.

Phyang, the small village in which the Chirpon family lives, is situated high in the Himalayas in a verdant valley, green with fields and trees, amidst an otherwise barren high-desert landscape. Their irrigation systems are intricately designed to conserve their most precious natural resource: water. Over a billion people inhabit the Himalayan river basins, and life in the region is sustained at every level by meltwater from the Himalayas.

Climate change, driven primarily by the carbon pollution of industrial superpowers far removed from small towns like Phyang, threatens to severely affect the glaciers of the Himalayas and reduce the water supply of the region. This growing water crisis will threaten the food security of an estimated 70 million people in the region by the year 2050.

The Chirpon family and millions like them whose lives are sustained through cultivation of that arid land will likely be among the first populations hit by the most destructive effects of climate change, yet they contribute the least to the problem. Meanwhile, the enormous fossil-fuel corporations responsible for warming the planet will be best positioned to adapt to climate change and continue to profit from the destruction.

As I began to wrap my head around the injustice of human-caused climate change, I reflected on what actions I could take personally. During the next two years, I grappled with the issue on several fronts. I took steps to reduce my own carbon footprint and water use, the biggest of which was becoming a vegetarian. I helped push my high school to begin recycling. I organized 5K races in my town to raise money for water projects in developing countries.

Then, in the summer of 2011, my perspective on climate change was completely transformed by an experience I had while visiting my old home in the North Cascades of Washington state. I took a backpacking trip with my older brother into what used to be our favorite part of the Glacier Peak Wilderness Area, Lyman Basin.

As we scrambled over boulders and crested the ridge to look out over Upper Lyman Lake for the first time in several years, we immediately knew something was seriously amiss. Lyman Glacier, sitting at the head of the valley, had retreated drastically against the mountain and the front of it had calved off into the water at its base. It was a surreal experience to see this glacier, upon which I remember having snowball fights in August as a child, so rapidly and irreversibly disappearing.

Abruptly, all those numbers and figures I held in my head about the Himalayan glaciers, which I had understood rationally, became real to me on a deeply disturbing emotional level. I had always thought of climate change as a problem for the future — something that would begin to be an issue in 50 or 100 years. As I stared at the exposed lines on the glacier, representing ages past — years, decades, centuries of winter snowpacks — climate change took on a far more personal urgency.

In the wake of that unsettling experience in Washington, I began to realize that individual behavior change — becoming vegetarian, recycling, changing light bulbs, and so on —would not be enough to prevent climate catastrophe, even on the largest scale.

That fall I began my first year at Harvard University, where courses in environmental science and public policy furthered my understanding of climate change. I joined protests against the Keystone XL pipeline proposal on campus, and bussed down to Washington, D.C. to surround the Whitehouse with thousands of others calling for President Obama to reject the pipeline.

What had become increasingly evident to me, and many others, was that the government needed to pass serious climate legislation to address climate change. But so far nothing was happening, and as our professors — most notably Naomi Oreskes — explained: the biggest reason for inaction is the disproportionate influence of the fossil-fuel industry over the political system and its widespread climate disinformation campaign.

This is Big Tobacco all over again, except instead of affecting susceptible individuals the fossil-fuel industry is ushering in a global crisis that will affect every being — rather than cancer of the lungs we're risking cancer of the entire planet.

As students before us had done in the face of Big Tobacco, as well as apartheid in South Africa and genocide in Darfur, we began a divestment campaign on campus to get Harvard to sell its fossil-fuel stocks and reinvest in socially responsible companies. Our campaign grew quickly; an undergraduate referendum showed 72% of college students in favor, and a Harvard Law School (HLS) referendum showed 67% of HLS students in favor. Over 1000 alumni responded to our call, along with more than 200 faculty members. But President Faust rejected the proposal to divest, and despite repeated calls from students and faculty she refused to engage in an open dialogue about divestment.

Our professors explained their climate research to us in classes and teach-ins, and it was terrifying. Their research made it clear that we are on a crash course with a catastrophe that has the potential to end life on earth as we know it and destroy the lives and livelihoods of millions of people. President Faust's assertion that Harvard's only role in fighting climate change would be through research, education and reduced consumption was intolerable for us — especially considering our classroom experience, where the teaching and research of our professors pointed us in the direction of divestment.

Because the fossil-fuel industry's influence in Congress was too great for Big Green NGOs to overcome on their own, we needed to build a mass movement to stigmatize those companies morally, intellectually, and politically in order to open up the political space for climate legislation to be passed. In response to President Faust's refusal to engage with the issue of divestment we decided to ramp up our tactics to match the scale of the climate crisis.

On a cold and rainy second night, protesters hold their ground at the main entrance to the ad building as police plan strategy.

So our blockade of Massachusetts Hall progressed. Freezing rain poured down, driving away most of the onlookers. Professors, alumni and community members rallied alongside us. Students from across Boston came to support the cause. We exchanged updates with divestment campaigners sitting in at Washington University, and got news that Stanford had announced its decision to divest from coal companies.

Activist groups organizing across the spectrum, from labor rights to sexual violence, joined us for an afternoon of sharing and discussing activism on campus. Major national news outlets reported on the events. Big climate organizations took notice and circulated a petition in support — 350.org, Energy Action Coalition, Rainforest Action Network and Forecast the Facts, to name a few. Over 65,000 people signed the petition calling on Harvard to divest.

As a dim dawn announced daybreak of our second day of blockading through the steady downpour, our energy was lifted as two Harvard chaplains emerged out of the rain and linked arms with us in the blockade. One of them was a former professor and a student leader in the South Africa divestment campaign decades ago.

But several hours later the police moved in once more, this time with handcuffs. They pried Brett off the main door far enough to secure access to the building, and whisked him off in a paddy wagon. We tried to continue holding our ground, but were shoved forcefully aside by police officers each time an administration member tried to enter. The blockade ended later that morning with no response from the administration to our demand for an open meeting.

The blockade had ended, but we emerged from it empowered both by the depth and breadth of support and the connection we experienced. It became clear to us that we were part of an increasingly cohesive national climate justice movement.

I share these experiences to demonstrate the deeply personal role of climate change in my life, and to demonstrate how inextricably involved I am as a principal — albeit a minor one — of the movement about which I research and write. My involvement in the movement on a personal level, as a co-coordinator of Divest Harvard and participant in many of the events about which I write, could raise the question of bias as I examine the movement from a scholarly perspective. However, there is a strong precedent for academic work of this nature, including the works of Howard Zinn's SNCC Snick: The New Abolitionists, *Jane Mansbridge's* Why We Lost the ERA *and Marshall Ganz's* Why David Sometimes Wins: Leadership, Organization and Strategy in the California Farm Worker Movement, *to name a few.*

~ ~ ~

Concurrently with his activism, Canyon's love of wilderness rivers and trails was recognized by his fellow students and he quickly became one of the leaders of the school's outdoor program during his undergraduate years at Harvard.

Taking his academic work at Harvard in stride with his passion for activism and outdoor adventure, Canyon graduated with honors from his department in May of 2015. During that summer, he became certified as a NOLS (National Outdoor Leadership School) instructor in kayaking, rafting and backpacking. Later he would guide river trips on the Salmon and Green Rivers.

The following spring (2016) he teamed up with his brother Forest to observe and film the Pacific Warriors' Conference in Fiji, a gathering of heads of state of the South Pacific island nations concerned with annihilation from rising sea levels as a result of climate change. Later, they filmed the devastation on individual islands. They will use these photographic records to promote greater awareness and action on this pressing global problem.

As one of the school's outdoor leaders, Canyon (right) shared his love of wilderness with hundreds of other students during his undergraduate years at Harvard. Father and son pause at Cloudy Pass while backpacking the North Cascades of Washington.

Canyon is rewarded for his fog-bound, early morning climb of Machu Picchu Mountain as, through breaking clouds, he meditates high above the ancient Inca city.

David

A Rainbow in the Storm

Darkness without hope.
The river wild awaits
Already it has laughed
With power sealed our fates.

Four boats set out this morn
Canyon filled with rain
Tonight there is but one
As to the wall we strain.

What's lost has flowed
On down the roaring tide
Left us wet and shivering
Upon the mountainside.

A pair upon these rocks
Two on the ledge afar
A torrent in between
No crossing of the bar.

But that one boat
With strokes so sure
Crossed to bring us back, to
Campfire's warmth once more.

So far removed
From all we know and love
The morning comes
And bids us, glance above.

A rainbow for a moment
Did pierce the darkest cloud
To fill our hearts with hope
Cast off the gloomy shroud.

A journey that was broken
Would come to life again
And defying somber odds
We'd ride the flow and win.

— Dad for David, whose kayak alone survived the untamed
Tatshenshini River

David is arguably the cutting-edge kayaker in a family of expert paddlers. Generous to all, whether on the river or in his own shop, he is respected and sought out for advice by other boaters in the Southeast. Craftsman, mechanic and outdoorsman, David has always been generous with his skills, ready to share with those in need. Many old friends and new river-runners appreciate that characteristic in him, choosing his companionship in unknown or dangerous whitewater runs.

I know of one kayaker, trapped in a swift water strainer on the Chattooga River, who owes his life to David's quick action. Running between Earl's Ford and Sandy Ford in high flow following two days of rain, Ron had veered perilously to the left of the safe route.

While other paddlers were still too far upriver to help in a timely manner, David saw what was about to happen, and quickly paddled his kayak to the downstream side of the log jam, yelling to Ron to lean into the mess in order to keep the current from grabbing and flipping the kayak.

Nevertheless, the boat was driven downward, Ron under water, until only the tip of the bow remained above the surface. David reached the jam immediately, grasped a log and abandoned his own kayak to the river. With his friend underwater, he knew that every moment was critical.

Then, with the same concentration that put him in control of our Yukon Territory adventure years before, he probed the strainer, pulled a gasping Ron free of his boat and the two of them into the closest safe eddy. One more potential river tragedy became simply a vivid river memory.

Again, on Overflow Creek, which is more a series of waterfalls than a typical creek, David — who recalls that, though he was above Singley's rapid and could not see what had happened to Ben, his fellow paddler below, heard an urgent voice in his head saying, "Throw the rope, jackass!"

David will swear to this day that the voice was that of his friend Chris, a kayaker who had passed away a year earlier. As it turned out, Ben was trapped beneath a rock undercut at the bottom of the rapid, a steep, near-vertical drop. The safety boat below could not pull the paddler from the undercut. But the blind rope toss was perfect, right into the trapped kayaker's grip, and the group was able to extract Ben without further mishap.

David leads as he and a young Forest challenge Jawbone Rapid in the Five Falls section of the Chattooga River. (David shown in inset.)

When each of his four younger siblings was born, it was David who was always there to make them welcome at their new home, a cheery fire in the woodstove and hot tea with a snack for Trish and myself. David's own words recall his growing years and their effect on who he is today:

I love to absorb the smell of the woods, the excitement in living water, and the friendships that arise from these experiences. Growing up as Doug's son has shown me that I am most comfortable when I am immersed in wilderness, particularly on a wild river where the path is only open to those who have the courage to challenge it.

I grew up among the many great whitewater paddlers that came from my father's coed explorer post, with countless hours spent in our basement creating kayaks, canoes and paddles. But the reward was the adventure that followed the birth of these boats.

In later years, I spent many hours patching boats, with and for friends, and giving them the opportunity to learn all aspects of

A songwriter and musician, David rarely travels without a guitar. Here, he plays for the family on the Grande Ronde River.

kayaking. Thankfully, the plastic kayak was born and the days of fiberglass splinters are over!

My father was always planning adventure in many forms. As a child, I did not necessarily share the enthusiasm of preparing for a trip, or even leaving, but once we were in the wilderness, living the adventure, everything changed and my spirit soon became tuned to the beauty and challenge of Mother Nature. The outdoors, and rivers in particular, are now the most important part of my life.

The outdoor lifestyle embodies independence and awareness. So, reflecting on the qualities that I see in the whitewater people that I know, they would be adventurous folk who enjoy planning a successful trip, are challenged by the river which they choose, and have the skills to rescue and help one another in difficult situations. They are a diverse group from all walks of life, ready to help the stranger in need as well as the friend.

I am fortunate beyond measure having a family with such a great love for the out-of-doors and for one another. If I needed help from any or all of them, they would be there in a moment. I feel that this close-knit group is a reflection of lifestyle and time spent adventuring together. I'm proud of each and every one of them, and look forward to the rest of life's great adventures together.

Cricket

Arctic Solitude

When silence roars
At the top of the world
And the river braids
Through channels old.

We stand together
On an island in time
The journey awaits
Your courage and mine.

'Tis only we three
No old guiding hand
To show us the way
Through this awesome land.

Alone, we savor
The pure mountain light
Caribou, bear and fox
Share each starry night.

Noatak, your essence
Our spirits did fill
To carry back with us
Direction and will.

Whether we return
Or no, you are
A part of our being,
Our river, our star.

— Dad for Cricket and the Noatak

Cricket, firstborn in her family generation, has embraced all of her siblings with love and open arms as each has appeared in her life. Raised in Maryland and Georgia, her heart was captured by the West on a family trip that included hiking in the Grand Canyon and Painted Desert. This was a huge factor in her choice of Colorado College for a biology degree, which served to reinforce her love of open, natural spaces. Now a professional photographer, musician and graphic designer, she has shared her skills with family and friends and has never stopped learning lessons of her own.

Early on, Cricket was drawn to horseback riding — an aptitude I never shared, despite my growing up on a farm. But she quickly took to horses, how to communicate with them and how to care for them. As a wrangler, she combined her love and knowledge of nature and horses to guide by horseback out of Santa Fe and packtrips by mule in the High Sierra for twelve years.

A veteran of many wilderness trips, including two family odysseys on rivers in Alaska, Cricket was also a rock climber for many years. Her macramé necklaces, embracing shark teeth and striking wilderness river stones, are

Cricket training in mounted archery in Oregon.

treasured by their wearers. A proponent of simplicity, she and her partner, Pete, are currently constructing a "tiny house" in Sisters, Oregon, which they will likely be living in by the time this book is finished. And, as I write these words, Cricket has recently returned from Mongolia, where she spent time photographing an international competition in horseback archery, a sport she enjoys participating in for its combination of horseback riding and martial arts (she has a black-belt in Tang So Do).

Cricket sings with her band, The Anvil Blasters, at a 2013 gig near Sisters.

When Cricket moved to Sisters, a talent she had only dabbled in previously was given the opportunity to mature. With a pleasing voice, and adept with fiddle, guitar and mandolin, she was offered a spot with the Anvil Blasters, and has now been a main-stay of the group for many years. The band is right out of the Old West and, as they advertise, their songs "...are peopled with border renegades and desert dreamers, poets and pirates, and ghosts of the old, weird America."

Her own words give us a bit of insight into the life and feelings that are hers in the high desert of Sisters, now her home:

As I write this, from my favorite spot in my mother's house, the window seat, my German-shepherd mix curled up on her end and watching the goings-on, I am delightfully distracted by the sounds of bird feet (corvids, most likely) gamboling across the roof.

The Stellar's jays (yup, corvids) then descend into the garden to glean things that I cannot see from the branches of the bushes. They poke into the bark mulch. Some venture into the lilac bushes and are abruptly chased into the junipers by the male black-headed grosbeak. Accusations fly. Again. And again. Many jays. One grosbeak. My lilacs! Indeed. It's his home and I'm guessing the female guards the nest.

I watch my mother walk to the end of the driveway to pick up the newspaper. She leans over to pluck a weed from the garden. The birds cease their bickering and sit quietly watching her.

My father loves being outdoors. In this way, I am more like my father. I studied biology in college because Nature's workings fascinate me. After graduation, I resisted tech jobs in laboratories, and instead guided trails by horseback in the Sangre de Cristos of New Mexico and the High Sierras of California. I framed art in Santa Fe in the winter.

Two women walk and talk on the neighborhood street a hundred yards away. I find myself wondering — with a noted touch of judgment — why some people walk and run on the asphalt and 55 mph roads near here when there are trails that lace the surrounding woods and ridges of our public lands so close. And I smile to recall an epiphany I had with my dad about 30 years ago.

I had just finished my second year of college, and Dad, Trish and Autumn, about a year old at the time, came out to Colorado to spend a week with me, backpacking in the Maroon Bells.

Trish and Dad took turns accommodating each others' and Autumn's needs, so this day saw Trish staying close to camp, or perhaps hiking a portion of the long trail that Dad and I hiked onto the shoulder of a peak. Then again, perhaps Trish was arranging personal time for Dad and me, which she does often, and I am grateful for her understanding.

So, Dad and I are sitting together on a high ridge in golden silence for the better part of an hour. Just watching. Gazing. Listening. Feeling the breeze on our skin and the magnificence in our hearts.

Dad breaks the silence with, "Thank goodness for New York City."

"What?!" I exclaim, baffled. I am so gullible. Still am.

He grinned with that giggly, slightly mischievous glint in his eyes and let me in on his thoughts: if Americans lived equally spaced over the surface area of our country — including all the mountains and Alaska just to demonstrate the idea — each person would have only a portion of an acre. No public land. No wildlands. Oh. I then agree: how wonderful that some people like to live on top of each other.

I had a dream about ten years ago, that a wildfire (that I was smelling as I slept) was spotting outside the cabin. In the dream, I put on my favorite pants, sweater, hat and boots, picked up my two photo albums, and walked out the door, dog right beside me.

In waking hours, I think I would add one thing to that list: my favorite stone from our Noatak river trip in Alaska. Somehow it may be the most treasured thing I "own." It fits in my hand perfectly, and has a thin line on the back that precisely matches a crease where it rests against my finger. I stroke it with my thumb and grand memories of that trip waft from my heart.

I have a dear friend whose house burned down years ago. He and his wife woke and carried their three daughters out of the house and watched it burn completely. He's the type to help others daily and had sent hundreds of photographs as postcards to friends and family through the years. After the fire, folks sent him back some of the letters, so that he again had a record of treasured memories. He shares his life connecting with everyone and everything around him, so he didn't really lose anything important.

I've heard that people nearing the end of life care the most about one thing: love. They ask themselves, "Am I loved?" "Did I love well?" From the way I spend my days, it seems that the shared love is too often a sideline activity, behind getting stuff done. What if shared love came first in every action of my day?

I've had the opportunity recently to examine my favorite memories. I see the patterns: hikes, walks, paddling, camping outdoors. Sharing time with family, good friends, dogs and horses. Laughing until I can't breathe. Traveling, from walks to journeys. Overcoming mishaps. Watching Nature's creations, admiring the innate knowing. Sparking wonder inside of me. Feeling included, valued, competent. Connected. I always feel this way outside with Nature. My ultimate favorite feeling: awe. I suppose that's my definition of love.

I rise from the windowseat and pad barefoot into the kitchen for more tea. An eagle is catching thermals in the canyon and circles to within a few feet of the kitchen window. Juvenile. The fledgling golden from the nest in the cliffs nearby perhaps. Lots of white on that rump. Maybe a juvenile from the nest of balds downstream? How graceful already at just a few months old! Oh, to fly instead of plod!

I admit, I am at times almost jealous of my younger siblings. Homeschooled. Outdoors even more than I am. Fluent in Spanish. Their experiences, friendships and cultural understanding through all their traveling. They have tapped deep wisdom about life at a much younger age than I have.

We have much in common: love of Nature, huge affection for each other, great compassion for others, practicality, goofy humor, lots of respect and gratitude. An understanding of self by reflecting in Nature.

The biggest difference that I see between myself and my home-schooled, well-traveled siblings is that they perceive less risk in life. Instead they see more possibilities. I attribute this to how Trish and Dad raised them: taking time slowly, exploring other lands and cultures, encouraging them to each follow their own curiosity. Ample opportunities to create — write, invent plays, express with art, play games — and most especially, time to care about what is happening around them and respond.

What I'm jealous of is that they are doing things that are signifi-cant. Things that I wish I were doing. Things that give me hope.

I am immensely proud of them. They do not worry as much as I do about how to make something they dream of happen. They just do it. They're creating lives they love. Not only do they speak out against injustice and destructive aspects of the status-quo, they do things about it. They risk arrest in protest. They organize and produce alternative-energy fairs. Participate in world peace projects. Travel alone in their teens to learn from researchers. They talk and work with big-time idea people, some whose names you would know. They volunteer all over the world. They are the change that they want to see. And they're still young! They are doing and will do so much to enrich the world and fill their souls!

The first flight of a baby bird from the nest. Is it afraid, or does it just know that it can fly? Is the risk that I perceive not even remotely in its being? What would it feel like to just lean out, reach into seeming nothingness and find that it holds me up?

~ ~ ~

As I write the final words for this book, Cricket continues to expand her art. She and Autumn, though geographically distant, just finished a collaboration on a powerful art project that was part of a 50-artist show in Bend, Oregon — an unusual accordian-style book they created with pieces of art each made and then transformed for the other: visually lifting each other's outlooks following their deep disappointment in our country's recent events. The project gave them and others hope and incentive to keep taking action for social justice, our environment and our quality of life.

"We placed the letter of hope that Dad wrote to all us kids — encouraging us to move beyond our disappointment in the 2016 presidential election — as part of this project. He gave us perspective of history he had lived through as an octogenarian, but that we had not experienced. He ended his letter with this encouragement: 'You — and many of your friends — have made a difference even at this point in your lives. Don't despair. Don't stop. Don't give up. Continue to give yourselves to the path that you know is right. We can't see around the dark corner in front of us, but the opportunities for action will appear. Seize them!'" — Cricket and Autumn.

Dreamer of Possibilities — Trish

Wild Heart

Out of sight on a rocky trail,
Down the river at a rapid pace
Eluding all who would follow,
She vanishes, leaving no trace.

Weeks in the cold Alaska rain,
Snow and wind in Lodore,
A lifetime of rivers, winding away
To a rocky, forbidding shore.

Oh no, never could she
Be content in Paradise.
No rest on our blue sphere as
She follows the moon in its rise.

She harasses the dragon,
That lays waste to our land.
A warrior of words, sharper than swords
Power cringes when she makes her stand.

Yet her soul is compassion itself
For those with a weaker voice
Who lack a shield or an advocate
Until she brings them that choice.

With a will of steel and a body to match
She climbs the trail while others fall
Refreshing the spirit of those who falter
Helping them over the wall.

She chose a partner years ago,
To share her trail as best he might
And guide four kids in ways of love
Forging paths that lead to light.

So here we stand, alone again
On a windswept mountain side,
That true wild heart, amazed that she
Still takes my hand, my love, my guide.

— Doug for Trish on our 32nd anniversary, June 27, 2013

There is, of course, one person who has shaped our family's story more than any other — my wife and partner — Trish.

It is she...

...who never lost the vision of family adventure — whether hiking a trail on our mountain at home or climbing to the ruins of Peru's lost cities.

...who started the books of personal letters that we wrote to each of our children through their early years.

...who fostered an environment of creativity around our children, teaching each to question the status quo, consider possibilities, and take action for change.

...who, when homeschooling support was nearly non-existent as Autumn reached school age, was instrumental in starting both local and statewide family support groups.

...who was, and is, the example of community engagement for our family in mentoring students in need, and bringing love and validity to the elderly who are confined to nursing homes.

...who continues to be the family catalyst, teaching by example when it comes to planning adventures, addressing thorny issues, and suggesting individual service projects that have meaning in our community.

...who could turn a normal gathering into a wild dance party in the blink of an eye or the toss of a water balloon!

~ ~ ~

No description of her is adequate, but I'll simply say, now as always, she holds this family together with love.

Debbie Clemons

Trish hiking in the mountains of North Carolina.

Spirited and out front on any issue of consequence, Trish was wearing a "Question Authority" T-shirt when she and I met in 1979. She has been questioning authority ever since — in a most informed and effective manner. When Trish sees an issue that needs to be addressed, she diligently researches the topic and moves forward with a plan of action, whether the issue be one of social justice or a threat to the environment.

She continues to be an advocate for young immigrants, as she has for the past ten years, tutoring them in language skills, and being instrumental in obtaining library access, entrance into early college and scholarships to summer camp for them. These kids, many of whom she has taught to swim, are frequently guests at our home for a swim party and campfire at the pond. The time around the campfire often gives rise to lively and serious discussions of issues that are on the minds of these inquisitive students.

Trish is a relationship builder, and besides her volunteer work, stays busy taking care of long-time friendships, as well as newer friendships made while traveling. Always the multi-tasker, Trish manages to balance her devotion to family and friends with organic gardening and outdoor sports, which keep her younger than her years. Paddle-boarding and swimming are high on her list of regular activities.

As she has for the past fifty years, Trish particularly enjoys engagement with the elderly of her community, absorbing their wisdom, colorful stories, and forming lasting friendships. Visits to local nursing homes and community meal delivery to those in need have established a rapport between Trish and those she serves that has a way of reaching back through time.

With endless possibilities for engaging with the suffering in the world, by loving and living life fully, Trish hopes to inspire others, through her actions and life, to take risks and blaze their own paths.

Trish and Doug

Trish and I still live in the mountain home that we built in the southern Appalachians more than thirty years ago, enjoying the rivers, trails and quiet country roads of this beautiful region. Almost at our doorstep, the Little Tennessee and Nantahala rivers often find us out for an afternoon paddle or an occasional overnight canoe trip.

With the Appalachian Trail visible from our mailbox, there is no way to resist its call and that of the many nearby trails for a hike to a favorite waterfall or to a spectacular view from the top of one of the numerous "balds" in the surrounding mountains. Likewise, the two of us still pack camping gear on our bicycles, taking off for a week on the backroads of Appalachia.

A piece of our hearts stays close to friends in Washington state and for a few weeks each year, we return to the tiny Stehekin cabin that we built in the North Cascades. The *Lady of the Lake* churns its way up the quiet lake to the small community at its head, friendships are renewed, and remote glacial valleys beckon us to once more hoist our backpacks and enjoy the isolation of true wilderness.

Even with our adult children traveling the world on their own paths, the "kids" often come home to relax and spend time with family — hiking a trail, camping on a river, or helping with a project at the home place, as well as sharing their own adventures with Mom and Dad.

In keeping with the values which drew us together nearly forty years ago, Trish and I retain a commitment to social justice for people of all persuasions, and to the protection of quality of life in our home mountains and far beyond.

Doug and Trish pause by a maypole in Tallberg, Sweden at the end of a six-day bicycle trip around Lake Siljan and nearby countryside in June of 2017.

Reprise

When I look back over the growing years of our family, now that the children are adults, I realize how much acceptance of the lives of others and appreciation of the ways in which nature works have formed their personal philosophies. Have they been consumed by a desire to accumulate wealth and immerse themselves in selfish comfort? I hope not. That would be a direction without meaningful purpose.

To a large degree, they have freed themselves from the artificial desires and maxims that our society imposes. Maxims that say: We must work endlessly to increase our income and then buy, buy, buy; that being a robust consumer takes precedence over a love of nature, music and art; that giving a gift of beauty to the world or another individual is a waste of time and energy.

They have been free to discover and evaluate without our rigidly saying, "This is the way it is." They have been free to make their own mistakes — and they have — and hopefully learn from them. They have been free to explore paths that we would never have chosen for ourselves.

What gives meaning to their lives? They would have to give you the definitive answer themselves, but from all that we have seen over the years, I would say this. Each of them has learned to approach life with an open heart for all beings, appreciating beauty, showing compassion and so bringing love into the lives of all whom they meet.

They know that we are but a small fragment of the natural environment in which we live. But that we, as humans, have the choice to affect that environment in a positive or negative manner. They continue to speak out, to write, to risk arrest for actions that they believe will help assure a future for their generation and beyond. They care deeply.

And perhaps most of all, they have been free to reach out, venture out, and finally embrace the fear of the unknown — to see through the distortions which our world and our leaders would have us believe as truth. To come to the realization that the creatures which inhabit the wild country of nature have as much right as we to enjoy life. To understand that other humans who have been demonized by our media and politicians just might have something worthwhile to teach us.

And, in trying to build the bridge over the unbridgeable chasm of our ignorance, we just might glimpse those on the other side who are trying to do the same. And somehow, when we meet in the center — with peril on all sides — the impossible becomes possible.

~~~

Appendix

Making it Happen

A Nod to the How
of Adventuring with Children

The Backcountry Adventure

Whether traveling by foot, bicycle or boat, it is always prudent to first take a day trip, then an overnighter, with the same gear which you expect to use on an extended trip with your little ones. How did the load feel? What necessary item(s) were you missing? Lay everything out when you get home, make a good evaluation of each item and see if it's really necessary and, if it is, could it be replaced by a simpler item which is smaller or weighs less.

You will find us giving advice from experience in backpacking, bicycle touring and whitewater paddling since these are the main areas to which our children have been exposed. Each of these disciplines requires differences in planning, particularly with food and cooking gear. In backpacking, you will want to mini-mize weight since it will all fall on the shoulders of the family. On bike trips, you have a little more leeway on weight, since your panniers and child trailer are "rolling stock." When canoeing, and especially when rafting, rivers, you can add "luxury items" if desired, since you will only be toting them to and from your campsites. Think twice, though, in lake country, where you may be portaging.

Certain considerations in planning will be the same, no matter what type of adventure you've chosen. Let's take a look, before we veer off toward a particular pursuit.

~ ~ ~

Clothing: Carrying the minimum clothing needed is always a challenge. However, children need more changes than adults, being prone to spills and slips around water. Nighttime in an arid climate, or an increase in elevation, can bring sharply cooler temperatures. Even in summer, we've always carried a full suit of fleece or pile for each child. This material retains warmth even when wet and dries quickly. Ours were all homemade, but children's clothing is now available commercially in a range of sizes for virtually any outdoor pursuit. Capilene underwear is excellent for warmth with minimal weight. A knit cap is essential for comfort since more body heat is lost through the head than anywhere else. Wool will hold heat in, even when wet. But be moderate when planning the children's everyday clothing — it's easy to over-pack!

Weather: Good waterproof raingear is essential for comfort in rainy or snowy conditions. This means a full set of jacket and pants for each child — our preference is Patagonia. A spare set of rain pants (ours are homemade) can go a long way toward preserving the underclothing of an infant in the crawling stage. For protecting an infant in a child-carrier, we recommend a poncho or backpack raincover (small size) adapted to fit over both the child and the carrier.

You're bound to get a variety of weather if you do much outdoors, but for safety and enjoyment, shift your dates, if possible, should the forecast appear to be blanketing your whole trip with foul weather.

Emergencies: The best scenario, of course, is to enjoy and complete your adventure without mishap. Thorough planning for your family's needs — taking into account individual abilities, terrain, adequate food and clothing, and the likelihood of wildfire, flooding and weather extremes — will go a long way toward eliminating emergencies.

However, even the best-prepared family will encounter the unexpected moment. Since many of your adventures will take place in wild country where medical assistance may not be at hand, it is essential that at least one of your family be trained in basic first aid, including CPR. This duty falls on the parents in the early years, but as the children become teens, they usually take an interest as well. All of ours have completed Wilderness First Responder certification as they continue to travel the rivers, trails and mountains of adventure.

Your children should know what to do in the unlikely event that they become separated from the rest of the family. That staying in place and waiting is usually the best course of action. How to best find or construct shelter in snow or violent rain. An excellent book that all of my children have read in later years is Laurence Gonzales' *Deep Survival*. The advice Gonzales gives addresses the emotional aspect of why some persons survive an unexpectedly crucial situation and why others just lose it and give up.

Be prepared! It is essential to know the whereabouts of the nearest hospital, EMS personnel or ranger for the territory in which you've chosen to travel, as well as a feel for the geography that you'll be in. This is particularly true if you're adventuring in a foreign country.

But remember, if you're in a wilderness area, you may not get a timely response from your GPS[7], or a signal from your cell phone. Much will depend upon your own knowledge and ability to act in an emergency situation. And it should go without saying, leave the electronic games at home.

You should be familiar with the wildlife that inhabits the area which you will visit. They are, whatever our prejudices may be, the permanent residents and, as such, deserve our respect. Almost without exception, the "scary critters" will go their way and disappear if we stay quiet and give them the chance.

---

[7] A GPS such as the DeLorme "In Reach" or the Spot "Messenger" can get a life-saving message to a source of help — just be aware of the time and terrain factors in actually getting that help to you.

This mother bear and her triplets are on their way to the historic apple orchard in Stehekin, WA. When you live on the edge of wilderness, sharing what you grow with wild animals can be both frustrating and necessary. Be sure to give these residents the respect and distance they deserve, and you'll find that they will do the same for you.

The Trail

These tips address the specific needs of a family backpacking with youngsters and are not expected to cover the total planning for a backpacking trip. If you are not already an experienced back-packer, we recommend that you read some of the many guides and periodicals devoted to the subject.

Conditioning: Take day hikes with your children in terrain similar to that in which you intend to backpack. Build enthusiasm toward the "overnighter" with these short fun trips as they condition their bodies to trail walking. Day-packs or fanny-packs filled with lunch and spare clothing — carried by the kids — will add to their sense of accomplishment. And it should go without saying that you need to be in shape, too!

Pace: Get an early start while everyone has a good supply of energy. Stop frequently, remove packs, eat a snack and drink plenty of water, even in the cooler seasons. Avoid hiking during naptime — unless your tiniest one is on your back (or front). Plan the hiking distance to suit the abilities of your most inexperienced family member. If you think it might be a drag gearing your pace down to that of your three-year-old, just remember that your own load is going to be 60 or 70% heavier than normal in order to meet family needs, and you'll probably welcome the shorter day!

Clothing: Diapers need to be planned carefully when they are called for. We usually carry six per day per child (we've only had one child in diapers at a time). Cloth can be rinsed (away from water sources) and dried for reuse on the trip. At nighttime, the extra absorbency of a disposable can be useful in keeping sleeping bags dry. Remember a plastic bag for carrying diapers out again.

Remember, in cooler weather, when carrying an infant on your back, she will need to be dressed more warmly than you since the heat you generate in hiking is not warming her!

In camp: (advice for kids as well as their parents) A loose-fitting, long-sleeved, light-weight shirt and a similar set of pants will help immensely during bug season, minimizing the use of repellent. Where mosquitoes and biting flies insist on keeping you company, a head net can provide welcome relief.

When our children have been infants and toddlers, we have shared our sleeping bags with them, both for added warmth and reduced trail weight. As they grew older, we added zip-in nylon ground sheets to make doubles, still pairing off, but with less weight than individual bags. We have always used bags with down fill, being careful to weatherproof them in packs. We've never regretted the choice of down.

Hanging food, at least 9 or 10 feet from the ground, either over a tree limb, or between two trees — but well away from the tree trunks and your sleeping area — should be routine for overnighters in the wild. Even if you are not in bear country, a number of smaller animals such as squirrels, opossums and raccoons can be attracted to the food scent. Check clothing pockets and tents for snacks, lip gloss, toothpaste and such before retiring. An unexpected food thief can spoil the trip for everyone!

When leaving camp for a day hike, even on the clearest of mornings, assume that rain will appear as soon as you leave, so make sure your tent's rain fly is in place and secure. Be sure to hang any food and toiletries that you're not taking with you, just as you would at night.

Be aware of regulations regarding campfires (are they prohibited, permitted only in designated fire rings, etc.) and use common sense as well. Never leave your site for any reason without making sure your fire is completely extinguished.

Footwear: Comfortably fitting, well-broken-in hiking boots, high enough to give ankle support are essential to the adults who will be carrying extra loads. So are smooth-fitting socks — wool or cotton as the season dictates. The same goes for the kids, except tennis shoes will suffice for the smaller children with light loads. Our preference is a pair of child's hiking boots worn and a pair of lighter shoes in the pack. Check at rest stops to make sure no one is getting a blister.

Clothing (adjust for season):

- Sun hat or visor
- Wool stocking cap or balaclava
- Rain gear (jacket and pants)
- Shorts and swimsuit
- T-shirts (non-cotton)
- Wool, fleece or pile shirts
- Fleece or wool pants
- Synthetic long underwear
- Underwear
- Synthetic-fill or down jacket

- Comfortable, well-broken-in hiking boots
- Socks
- Camp shoes
- Gloves
- Diapers with bag for carrying them out
- Towel

Personal Equipment:

- Backpack, with adjustable waist, shoulder and chest straps, sized to fit the wearer.
- Lightweight fanny-pack or day-pack, for day trips away from base camp (some backpacks have a detachable top flap that becomes a fanny-pack)
- Lightweight first aid kit (see separate listing below)
- Snack bag (small stuff-sack) to carry items needed during the day (camera, sunscreen, matches, snacks, etc.)
- Sleeping bag
- Sleeping pad
- Tarp or tent with poles & stakes
- Stuff-sacks, compression sacks, as needed
- Headlamp for each person, with spare batteries
- Personal items (toothbrush, toothpaste, hand lotion, glasses or contacts, towel or washcloth, biodegradable soap, razor, etc.)
- Notebook and pen
- Knife, matches, fire-starter (best if carried on your person)
- Water bottle
- Water filter, Steri-pen, or chemical water purifier
- Insect repellent

- Lip balm
- Sunscreen
- Sunglasses with safety strap
- Camera, with lenses, etc.
- Emergency whistle
- Trail maps
- Compass
- Food bag that can be hung
- Small-diameter nylon cord (70 ft) for hanging food bag
- Plastic trash bags (for carrying out trash, and for protecting gear from rain, if not otherwise protected)
- Toilet paper

First Aid Kit — Lightweight:

- Moleskin for blisters on hands or feet
- Assorted Band-Aids
- Butterfly closures
- Ace bandage
- Ibuprofen
- Liquid children's Tylenol
- Snake-bite kit
- Tweezers
- Personal medications (if you carry drugs, work with a doctor to learn correct dosages and possible side effects)

Cooking and Food Equipment:

- Small stove and fuel
- Lightweight stainless pots (as required for menu)

- One lightweight cup, plate/bowl and one spoon per person
- Food and spices

The River

Have you ever driven alongside a beautiful river, watching it twist and turn, rush over ledges, and then suddenly leave your view, disappearing into wild country? As a child, I often gazed out of a car window and wondered into what magical country that waterway might carry me. As I grew into adulthood, the siren call continued and I began to follow those rivers to see where they might lead. I was never disappointed.

As a parent, it was natural to introduce my own children to these experiences, to see if they shared my longing and enthusiasm for remote river country. They did. All six of them. The early steps were safe and easy ventures onto slow-moving but pristine creeks, later adding camping to the mix, and eventually challenging the whitewater rivers of our American Northwest and Alaska with week-long and even two-week trips.

How young a child can you take down the river? That depends on the attitude of both parent and child, as well as the difficulty of the river itself. As a parent, do you feel comfortable with your own paddling skills on the chosen river? Are you canoeing, kayaking or rafting? Each can offer an incredible experience for the child, but generally a raft — high quality and sized to the family — will accommodate more gear and more family members on a multi-day trip.

We spent a week on the Green River in Colorado and Utah when our youngest was only seven months old. Most importantly, we were familiar with the river, knowing that Trish could carry Canyon around the most difficult rapids, including Hell's Half Mile, while I ran the raft through. Guidebooks (available at local outfitters and park offices) are a must for river-running, but previous first-hand experience is even better.

When it comes to equipment, a life-jacket (or personal flotation device (PFD), as it is know today) is a must for all paddlers, but particularly so for infants and toddlers. The first requirement is that the PFD be able to turn the small child face up, no matter what position she was in when entering the water. Secondly, there should be crotch straps to prevent the PFD from sliding up and coming off over the head. Third, there must be enough buoyancy in the PFD to keep the child's head comfortably above the surface, even in moving water. Bright PFD colors are preferable for keeping an eye on your child when she is playing near the water's edge in camp. NEVER strap the child in a carrier or fasten her in any way to the watercraft, even on a tether. She should be free-floating in case of a capsize.

Campsites can be intriguing playgrounds for young river travelers. Are there trails where the family can take hikes suited to the energy of the youngest member? Is there a small side creek where stones can be rearranged into dams and channels by small hands? Are there rocks that can be safely climbed? Is there wildlife that can be observed? Our son Forest once saw a ground squirrel scamper away with one of his matchbox cars. The wonder of what was happening overcame his sense of loss!

With raft trips, you are able to carry a bit more equipment — gear that you would never take on a backpacking or bicycle journey, or even on a canoe or kayak trip. Since everything revolves around water, bring that third or fourth set of warm clothing along for the kids, just in case. Rain jacket and rain pants are essential, not just for the weather, but for splashes that will come over the sides of your canoe, kayak or raft.

No matter what your choice of watercraft, medium or large waterproof dry bags are necessary for protecting clothing, diapers, sleeping bags, pads and food from splashes, rainfall or capsizes. A small waterproof "day bag" will be handy for keeping sun screen, lip balm, camera, kids' snacks, and similar items at the ready. Each person, including your kids, should have a water bottle available during the time on the river. If you are traveling by raft, chances are that your main food supply will be kept in a large cooler and a dry box.

Does your chosen river require a permit? More and more, we are required to bow to bureaucracy in order to enter our favorite wild places. However, the other side of this means that the permit — as restrictive as it may be — is there to assure an uncrowded wilderness experience where there will be little competition for camping spots and you will have a good chance of enjoying the solitude for which you came.

Some rivers require only an on-the-spot, register-at-time-of-launch permit, while the more popular ones entail entering a lottery, where the chance of winning a launch date is relatively slim. If you don't know the procedure for the river you have in mind, check with a nearby outfitter or, better yet, the controlling agency — U.S. Forest Service, National Park Service, Bureau of Land Management, etc. If you are really fortunate, your river may be one which requires no permit.

Much more than the trail or the road, a river is a living, changing entity. Too little water can turn your river adventure into a boat-dragging, foot-bruising, slippery hike — one which your little one will not remember fondly, particularly when you are overtaken by nightfall at some inhospitable bend of the river. On the other hand, high water can turn your trip into a life-threatening nightmare, and is no place for yourself, let alone small children.

That said, rivers rated Class 3 or less usually have a range of water levels within which it is quite safe to navigate. Most rivers in the U.S. are classified on a scale of one through six in difficulty, an exception being the Colorado River, which is fine-tuned on a scale of one through ten. You also want to know what individual hazards — such as a dam or a rapid rated significantly higher than the overall rating for that river, might be encountered. American Whitewater (americanwhitewater.org) can supply water level information for almost any river in the United States. They can also tell you which rivers need permits and whom to contact to apply for one.

If this advice — for your first river experience — sounds over-whelming, consider taking your family down the river with an outfitter. The trip will free your mind from many of the logistics, allow you to concentrate on the needs of your children, and give you a feel for handling future details on your own.

The Woodward family rafting the Grande Ronde River on a misty Oregon morning.

BOATS AND ACCESSORIES:

Rafts: Most forgiving, but slowest-moving, of river craft; can carry the most gear.

- Inflatable raft of high-quality material; self-bailing with at least four separate air chambers (recommend NRS line)
- Life jackets (PFDs) for all, plus one extra per raft**
- Pump

- Rowing frame & oars, if a single person is to row. Straps for lashing frame to raft; oar locks; oar stops; spare oar — *or*, if all are to participate: paddles for everyone, plus a spare
- Bow & stern lines
- Repair kit (see kit details below)
- Waterproof bags and/or rigid containers to carry gear and food
- Bailing buckets if raft is not self-bailing
- Plenty of straps and carabiners for lashing gear above floor of raft
- An accessible water bottle for each person
- Tarp or cargo net to cover equipment on raft

Open Canoes: Require more paddling skills than rafts; faster and more maneuverable than rafts; gear and kid space is more limited than rafting.

- Canoe (lake or whitewater), sized to accommodate supplies and occupants
- Paddles for everyone (small ones for kids), plus a spare
- Life jackets (PFDs) for each person**
- Bailer (a gallon milk jug with end cut out makes a good one)
- Bow & stern lines
- Sponge for mopping up small splashes
- A roll of duct tape for immediate repairs
- Waterproof bags to carry gear and food
- Flotation bags (waterproof gear bags will provide limited flotation if gear space is tight)
- Plenty of straps for securing gear in canoe
- An accessible water bottle for each person

Kayaks and decked canoes: Require more specialized paddling skills than rafts or open canoes; faster and more maneuverable than either; gear space is more limited, although sea kayaks provide greater space than river kayaks; kids will need to be older to paddle their own kayaks solo.

- Kayak or decked canoe
- Life jacket (PFD) for each paddler**
- Paddle
- A spare break-down paddle
- Flotation bags
- Small, waterproof bag for readily accessible items
- Sponge
- Spray skirt
- Helmet
- A roll of duct tape for immediate repairs
- Wetsuit or drysuit
- Wetsuit booties
- Mittens, pogies, hood if paddling in cold weather or water
- Paddling jacket if no drysuit
- Rescue bag (throw rope)
- An accessible water bottle
- River knife attached to life jacket

**Pay particular attention to your choice of children's life jackets. For infants and toddlers, passive head support above water is critical. Usually, it takes a full flotation collar (360°) rather than a behind-the-head flap to achieve this. Older children will match their weight to a particular life jacket size. Always give your child and her life jacket a pre-river trial in safe water.

REPAIR KIT (required by many permitting agencies):

Common to raft, canoe or kayak trips:

- Duct tape (the universal temporary repair material)
- Rag for drying area to be repaired

Specific to multi-day or demanding raft trips:

- Patching material, glue, solvent (all items should be compatible with materials used in your raft)
- Scissors to cut patching material
- Brush to apply glue
- Sandpaper
- Carpet thread or dental floss, and carpet needle to mend bad tears

Raft with a frame would also include:

- Tools (vise-grips, pliers, screwdriver, wrench, hand drill & bits, hammer, small saw)
- Wire (soft and flexible)
- Pipe clamps
- Extra screws, bolts, nuts, nails, washers to fit parts on frame
- Epoxy
- Replacement parts for any breakable item

FIRST AID KIT:

- Triangular bandages
- Gauze rolls (two inches wide)
- Moleskin for blisters on hands or feet
- Assorted Band-Aids
- Sterile pads (four by four inches)
- Butterfly closures
- Safety pins
- First aid tape (two-inch size)
- Ace bandage
- Aspirin
- Ibuprofen
- Liquid children's Tylenol
- Antacid tablets
- Allergy tablets, such as Benadryl
- Snake-bite kit
- Tweezers
- First aid book
- Personal medications (if you carry drugs, work with a doctor to learn correct dosages and possible side effects)

CLOTHING:

Choose your paddling clothing and equipment (that fit the type of river trip you will be taking) from the previous list, plus the following:

- Sun hat and/or helmet, depending on water difficulty
- Windbreaker or paddling jacket
- Rain gear (jacket and pants)

- Shorts and swimsuit
- T-shirts (non-cotton)
- Wool, fleece or pile shirts or jackets
- Fleece or wool pants
- Synthetic long underwear
- Underwear
- Synthetic-fill or down jacket
- Wool stocking cap or balaclava
- Camp shoes
- Gloves for camp

PERSONAL EQUIPMENT:

- Waterproof bag (large) to carry personal clothing & equipment
- Waterproof bag (small or medium) to carry items needed during the day (camera, sunscreen, matches, snacks, etc.)
- Sleeping bag
- Sleeping pad
- Tarp or tent with poles & stakes
- Headlamp with spare batteries
- Personal items (toothbrush, toothpaste, hand lotion, glasses or contacts, towel or washcloth, biodegradable soap, razor, etc.)
- Eating utensils (cup, spoon, plate, fork & spoon)
- Notebook and pen
- Knife, matches, fire-starter (best if carried on your person)
- Water bottle (should be available in boat)
- Insect repellent
- Lip balm

- Sunscreen
- Sunglasses with safety strap
- Fishing gear and fishing license
- Camera with lenses, etc.

SAFETY AND RESCUE EQUIPMENT:

- Life jackets (as previously mentioned)
- Throw-rope rescue bags or ropes in each boat
- Signal mirror (on extended trips in remote country)
- Emergency whistle for each person
- *On difficult wilderness rivers:* winch, carabiners, slings, prusiks

OTHER GROUP EQUIPMENT:

- Waterproof river map(s)
- Compass
- River guidebook and area resource books
- Drinking-water containers (5 gal/day/6 persons)
- Large-capacity filters or other means of water purification
- Permit for river, if required
- Matches and fire-starter
- Ropes for lining boats
- Small folding shovel
- Lantern (4 "D" batteries)
- Fire pan with grill
- Plastic garbage bags
- Burlap bags or nylon stuff-sacks to use over plastic garbage bags to prevent spills (also handy for carrying cooking pots, Dutch ovens, fire pan)

- Toilet paper
- Portable toilet system (known as the "groover," and consisting of toilet seat and spill-proof vault — usually a 5-gal rocket box)
- A few "wag bags" as an extension to the groover, for emergency individual use when groover is not set up
- Lightweight folding chairs for comfort in camp, if desired

COOKING AND SERVING EQUIPMENT:

Lightweight trips:

- Pots
- Small stove and fuel
- One cup and one spoon per person
- Food and spices
- Several lighters

Luxury-style trips, add:

- Dutch oven, with firepan
- Charcoal briquettes (Kingsford Original work best) for dutch oven, or when wood is scarce
- Frying pan
- Coffee pot
- Griddle
- Buckets to gather wash-water from river
- Coolers and other food containers
- Spatula
- Large spoons
- Pliers for handling hot lids

- Pot-holders
- Kitchen knives
- Small cutting board
- Can opener
- Burlap bags to hold Dutch ovens and pots
- Propane or gas stoves (if fires are not used), with appropriate fuel
- Paper towels
- Cloth dish towels
- Plastic dish tubs: 1 wash, 1 rinse, 1 bleach
- Dish soap and scrubber
- Bleach for sterilizing dishes and utensils
- Eating utensils for each person
- Food and spices
- Folding or roll-up table(s)

The Byway

Is bicycling your forte? Bike touring? Do you ever picture yourself traveling this way with your children, turning off to explore an inviting byway, stopping to see what that farmer is doing, having a conversation with the family at the picnic table, all of this made possible simply because you are on bicycles?

The Woodward family prepares to leave their North Carolina valley on a two-night shakedown trip, checking out equipment before departing for a month of biking in the rural areas of England and Wales. Left to right: Autumn, Doug, Rivers, Forest, Trish and Canyon.

The road starts at your doorstep. It can connect you with any other road, anywhere on your continent. Well, almost. Various islands and communities like Stehekin require a few more logistics!

That said, your choices normally will be myriad. But how safe is bicycle touring as a family mode of travel? No path in life comes with a guarantee, but with good planning you can reduce the risk of mishap to a minimum. Are there dedicated bike paths, bike lanes, or ample shoulders on the route you would take? Are the roads heavy traffic arteries or do they receive light use? Will there be campgrounds available when you need them, such as the hiker/biker-only sites along the Oregon Coast? The local department of transportation and chambers of commerce will usually have the answers to these questions.

Although we had never bike-toured before Trish and I married, it quickly became a way of life for us from the time our first child could hold her head up in a bike seat, right through the progression of our four children's growing years. When I say "progression," I'm referring to "age and ability-sensitive modes" of bike travel, which change over the years as the kids grow older. (i.e. — child seat, child trailer, tandem bike, individual bike matching child's size.)

A tandem bike makes a good transition from being pulled in a child trailer to a young one riding her own bike. A child crank extension allows Autumn's legs to reach the pedals from the stoker seat.

When our children were infants or toddlers, they traveled in a bike seat right behind mom or dad. We also pulled a child trailer behind my bike, where two kids could snuggle in, look at books or take a nap in rough weather, while Mom and Dad did the heavy lifting. As they grew, they graduated to the tandem, taking the stoker (rear) position with a child crank to accommodate the shorter legs. At age eight or nine, the transition would be made to a bike of their own, slightly smaller (24-inch wheels) than ours, but with a rear rack and lightly loaded set of panniers.

How much distance can you cover, your bike carrying full panniers front and rear, and pulling a loaded child trailer? We found that in moderate mountain terrain, 5 to 6 miles per hour was doable; in rolling hills, 6 to 8 mph, and in relatively flat territory, 8 to 10 mph. However, don't simply divide those figures into your map distance. Remember, when traveling with children, you should spend at least as much waking time off of the bikes as on. Stop to wade in the creek, play a game, read a short story, and of course to eat lunch.

There will come times, of course, when you have to churn down the road without a normal break — the temperature is plummeting, the rain is closing in, a child is feeling ill — but these are more the exception than the rule.

What kind of bicycle should you use? A road bike? Mountain bike? Hybrid? To some degree, this choice will depend on the terrain over which you expect to ride, but when biking

Rail Trails — old railroad beds that have been converted to biking and hiking paths — are usually safe and friendly places for children to try out their new biking legs on day or overnight adventures. Left to right: Rivers, Trish, Autumn, Forest.

with small children, reliability also becomes a larger factor. You'll want to keep the break-downs to a minimum, and to do this, we — through our own experience — found that the mountain bike was rugged enough to handle extra child and gear weight without popping spokes on an English bridle path or trashing a wheel bearing when we were 100 miles from a bike shop.

As happened with covered wagon travel heading west in our country a century and a half ago, you will find that you tend to bring more than you really need when starting out. Along the Oregon Trail, since most of the route was uninhabited, items deemed as "excess baggage" simply got tossed to the side when the over-loaded wagons and the mules and oxen pulling them bogged down.

Your legs, also, will likely tire of struggling up hills, pulling baggage that you may never use. If your trip is due to last several weeks, you will want to have a shakedown day early-on, to give away, or mail home, items that you determine are not necessary to the remainder of the journey.

Rail or bus travel can be a good option for traveling from one biking area to another when you want to avoid traffic congestion or long stretches of desolate country with your children. Make sure, ahead of time, that your carrier will take your equipment aboard, as well as what restrictions might apply to this mode of transport.

Clothing (adjust for season): for both children & adults unless noted otherwise:

- Helmet & visor
- Wind jacket
- Wool stocking cap or balaclava
- Rain gear (jacket and pants)
- Shorts and swimsuit
- T-shirts
- Wool, fleece or pile shirts
- Fleece or wool pants
- Synthetic long underwear
- Underwear
- Synthetic-fill or down jacket for camp
- Shoes — comfortable cross-trainers (use for both biking and in camp) or dedicated, self-locking bike shoe
- Socks
- Gloves
- Diapers with bag for carrying used ones
- Towel

Personal Equipment:

- Bicycles (as required by family size and ages) — adult mountain bikes (26" or 27" wheels), with pannier racks, and geared extra-low for climbing under load; youth mountain bikes (24" wheels) with rear pannier rack; child trailer with rain cover and safety markings.
- All bikes should be equipped with LED tail lights (with a flashing setting) and front LED headlamps for road safety.
- Paniers, waterproof preferred. Definitely a rear pair, and probably a front pair also, when traveling with kids. We

288 You Took the Kids Where?

found it efficient to pack our down bags and sleeping pads in a medium waterproof river bag and bungee it across the rear panniers, helping to hold them in place on bumpy terrain.

- Lightweight fanny-pack or day-pack, if day hikes away from camp are anticipated.
- First aid kit (see separate listing of contents below)
- Handlebar bag to carry items needed during the day (camera, sunscreen, journal, snacks, etc.)
- Sleeping bag
- Sleeping pad
- Tarp or tent with poles & stakes
- Stuff-sacks, compression sacks, as needed
- Headlamp for each person, with spare batteries
- Personal items (toothbrush, toothpaste, hand lotion, glasses or contacts, towel or washcloth, biodegradable soap, razor, etc.)
- Notebook and pen
- Knife, matches, fire-starter
- Water bottles (2 in bike cages, 1 in pannier rear pocket, for each bike)
- Water filter, Steri-pen, or chemical water purifier if camping in primitive sites
- Insect repellent
- Lip balm
- Sunscreen
- Sunglasses with safety strap
- Camera, with lenses, etc.
- Maps showing roads, trails and camps
- Food bag that can be hung (if primitive camping)
- Small-diameter nylon cord (70 ft) for hanging food bag
- Plastic trash bags (for carrying trash, and for protecting

gear from rain, if not otherwise protected)

- Toilet paper

First Aid Kit:

- Triangular bandages
- Gauze rolls (two inches wide)
- Moleskin for blisters on hands or feet
- Assorted Band-Aids
- Sterile pads (four by four inches)
- Butterfly closures
- Safety pins
- First aid tape (two-inch size)
- Ace bandage
- Aspirin
- Ibuprofen
- Liquid children's Tylenol
- Antacid tablets
- Snake-bite kit
- Tweezers
- First aid book
- Personal medications (if you carry drugs, work with a doctor to learn correct dosages and possible side effects)

Cooking and Serving Equipment:

- Small stove and fuel
- Lightweight pots (as required for menu)
- One cup, plate, fork & spoon per person
- Food and spices

Learning from the World

As we've mentioned earlier, your family's first adventure should be one with which you're comfortable, and this advice certainly applies to travel beyond the borders of your own country.

Unless you are already fluent in another language, or are traveling with someone who is, countries whose residents speak your own language will be your obvious first choice. This will allow you to make reservations, field passport questions and easily shift plans as you go.

Do you have a friend who has been to the country or region that you are considering visiting? Or, better yet, do you know someone who is a native of that country, or has lived there for a period of time? Picking her brain can be a tremendous help, both in your planning and in overcoming fear of the unknown.

Down-to-earth guidebooks, such as the *Lonely Planet* series, are also invaluable planning tools. Pick your destination, and almost any country you choose will have an on-line traveler's blog that can fill you in on the latest ways to travel locally, campgrounds and bargain places to stay, spots to avoid, and a host of answers to questions you haven't yet thought to ask. Most sites are interactive, so ask your own questions, too.

When traveling in a new country, keeping the kids happy and interested is paramount to the experience that they will bring home, as well as their enthusiasm for next time. Seek out the children's parks in the small towns — they are great places for making friends, both young and old. Find out what snacks the shops carry and be sure the snacks are readily available when your kids are confined to a bike seat or trailer.

If possible stay away from those places that are crowded with tourists. Resist the urge to hang out with other travelers of your own nationality or race. Your image will be quite different when you travel openly — by bike, foot or local transportation. Let the locals know that you are there to interact. Ask questions. Show them photos from home. Children are instant icebreakers. They will spontaneously connect with other children and join in games.

Bringing small gifts that can be easily slipped into our packs is a courtesy to friends with whom we share time, particularly when we enjoy their food or spend a night under their roof. Small flashlights, photos of our family and postcards showing our home area have all been well received. And when we are guests for longer periods of time, we always arrange to pay for the services of our hosts.

Occasionally, we might have the opportunity to cook for our host family. When we think that this could occur, we plan ahead by bringing a few simple recipes whose ingredients are available locally and will not require an array of cooking gear. And we are aware that we may be served items which seem strange to our palates, yet are considered a delicacy in the host country, reserved for honored guests. If a roasted guinea pig appears on your plate, you will know that you are at the top of your host family's favored list. Smile, eat and thank them!

And be sure to keep a journal of your travels. Years from now, it will refresh your memory, provide contact information for friends made along the way and point the way as your children grow into their own style of travel.

When we travel abroad, there are certain preparations that we make before leaving home. These are commonsense precautions to keep — as much as possible — unpleasant situations from detouring an incredible family experience. Your own travel situation may dictate differences, but here's what we normally do:

- Obtain **passports** for general travel outside of your home country. In the U.S., allow six to eight weeks for the processing of a new passport. Be sure that you have the required documentation for birth, residency and citizenship, as well as photos in the specified size and format.

- A **visa** for the country to which you are traveling (if a visa is required for that country). A visa may be obtained from the local embassy for that particular country. There are visa agencies (not the embassy) who specialize in rush processing of visa applications for an additional fee. You will need a valid passport before applying for a visa.

- Check for **entrance and exit fees** for the country(s) to which you are traveling. These are usually paid at the airport or border crossing as you enter or exit.

- Use a **travel pouch** that remains inside your clothing at the belt line for main cash, passport, cards, and a copy of your emergency information.

- Take only **essential credit and debit cards** and be sure to let your bank and credit card companies know that you will be using your cards in another country so that they don't put a hold on them.

- Carry your **driver license** for additional ID and if you intend to drive in the destination country. Most countries accept driver licenses from the traveler's home country rather than requiring an International Driver License, but it's best to check if you intend to drive while traveling.

- Contact your health insurance company for foreign travel requirements before you leave. Take your **health insurance card** if it could be useful. Most companies insure you in countries away from home, but will only reimburse you when you return. If you are in a country that speaks a different language, the bill must be translated to your home language and currency before reimbursement.

- For **health conditions, immunizations** required, restricted areas, etc. in any country, call the **CDC** at 404-CDC-INFO or go to cdc.gov/travel. If you don't immunize, there is usually no difficulty traveling from the U.S. to another country and then returning. But when you are traveling through several different foreign countries, you could be barred from entering one without showing a "yellow card" as proof of specific immunizations.

- Use a lightweight **"decoy" wallet** that contains only the estimated cash needed for that day and nothing else.

Before your trip, you will want to take the time to assemble a comprehensive travel information sheet (usually two or three pages) and make several copies, one to leave with family or trusted friends at home, others to carry with you, in luggage or clothing apart from your passport and other vital documents. This measure will be invaluable should any of your travel documents be lost or stolen.

Information we like to have on our travel sheet is:

- **Photocopies of passports, driver licenses and all cards**. Be sure to copy both sides of credit cards, since the back shows the number to call if a card is lost or stolen. However, block out all but the last four digits of cards (including the image that shows through to the back) since this, and your name, is enough to identify the card if it has to be cancelled, but not enough for a thief to use.
- **Contact information** (email and phone) for any known contacts in your **visited countries**.
- **Contact information** (email and phone) of friends and relatives at **home**.
- **Airline itinerary**: dates, times, flight numbers, and record locators for air travel to and from the U.S.
- **American Embassy contact info** for the countries in which you are traveling. www.usembassy.gov or call the State Dept. at 202-647-5225, to obtain info.
- A **list of English-speaking doctors** in the countries in which you are traveling. IAMAT.org or call 716-754-4883 ahead.
- **CDC** contact information cdc.gov/travel to assess health conditions while traveling should you have questions.
- **Phone numbers and email addresses of the airline(s)** with whom you are flying, both in your home country and the countries you are visiting.

- **Phone numbers and email addresses of any surface transportation** (rail, bus, ferry, etc.) on which you may expect to travel.

- **Phone numbers and email addresses of inns, hostels and campgrounds** at which you might stay. We always reserve ahead, a place to stay on the night of our arrival, but usually leave the rest of our itinerary open.

- **Phone numbers and email addresses** of any folks who will be **local contacts** in your destination country, such as proprietors of places to stay, friends of friends at home, etc.

- **Any other information** which you feel could be vital to the functioning of your trip.

That's a heap of logistics to include on your travel information sheet, but if you find yourselves in a bind — like a lost passport — it can save you many headaches.

Leave a copy of the above list with your home contact person, another with a trusted new contact person (either known ahead of time or chosen after your arrival) in the visited country. Make sure a copy travels with each family member, children included, in an item of his or her luggage.

In our early travels, we depended on Internet cafes for communication. They are in decline now, with WiFi almost universally available. The smartphone has thus become the preferred tool of travelers for Internet needs and, in many cases, voice communication.

The great majority of folks that you will meet in your travels will be honest and helpful, and will go out of their way to make your experience an outstanding one — despite language barriers. Nevertheless, being alert and avoiding crowded places, keeping your pack always in sight (better yet, in your lap) when traveling, being aware of deliberate distractions, and using common sense all go a long way toward minimizing unpleasant situations.

Have we ever been robbed? Yes. We were in a country that we considered "safe" compared to others in which we had spent time. We were too relaxed, deliberately distracted by a man speaking rapidly in Spanish in order to draw our attention his way while his accomplice worked, and Autumn's fanny-pack vanished into thin air. There was nothing in it of value to the thief (we don't carry cash in fanny-packs), only the one item which meant the most to her — her day-by-day journal of the trip, with contact information of the friends she had made. Thus the list of precautions, taken both before and during travel.

But there can be unexpected rewards for being in an unfamiliar country. On a Friday evening in Cuzco, Peru, at 11,000 ft elevation, I noticed slight discomfort in one of my molars. "Unequalized pressure from the altitude change," I thought. By late Saturday afternoon, however, the intensity of the pain had built to a point where I knew it was not going away without help. "Isn't this always the way — right in the middle of the weekend," I despaired.

But our friends weren't fazed in the least. "There are four dental clinics within a twenty-minute walk of our home," volunteered Chachi. "But it's Saturday night," I countered. "Then they'll close at ten," she replied. We went. The dentist and her nurse could not have been more competent. Modern equipment. Professional diagnosis. X-rays. Pain prescription. Root canal needed. And yes, the pharmacy across the street was still open. All this at a tenth of the cost in the U.S.

~ ~ ~

By studying up-to-date travel guides, such as the Lonely Planet series, you can get a grasp of costs for hostels, campgrounds, food, and bus or rail travel. Plan your budget carefully, and decide how you will handle money — through a debit card, credit card, cash or a combination. Travelers checks are now ancient history. If you count on a debit card and home bank account for the source of most of your funds, *make sure that two of you each have a card with different numbers, so that one will still be able to access your account,* should you have to cancel the other because of loss or theft.

We change a small amount of home funds into the currency of the destination country at our airport of departure. Know the exchange rate, so that you can approximate the correct transaction in your head — better yet, carry your own calculator. Often, you will find that independent money changers in the destination country give a better rate than banks or airports. But make sure they have at least a tiny office, not a back alley.

If you are a SERVAS traveler (see page 5), be sure that you have your letter of introduction and the directory of host families for the country in which you are traveling.

If you are couch surfing, use the appropriate Internet information. Couch-surfing is a free world-wide network of hosts and travelers, but hosts can rarely accommodate families. See couchsurfing.com.

What we don't do before leaving, however, is plan our whole itinerary. To do so, we feel, would limit the spontaneity of the experience. It is reassuring, though, particularly with young travelers, to know where you will be on the day/night that you arrive. In our case, it is usually a hostel or modest guest house, recommended by a friend or carefully chosen from the guidebook. From that point on, we can move in directions of our own choosing, based on what we see or learn locally.

An often-asked question is, "How do you find the folks that you visit in other countries?" Contact at home with exchange students, or friends who are native to that country can help, but most often it is the language schools in the visited country that will connect you with home stays and immersion experiences. An Internet search will put you in touch with these excellent sources.

Returning to Peru in January of 2014, Canyon and Trish walk toward the cloud-covered peaks beyond the ruins of Moray.

Acknowledgements

When your gaze wanders back toward the paths that cover a time span as lengthy as these pages, you realize how many folks have contributed to the effort – not just in the creation of the book itself, but in the experiences which made it possible.

Trish, my wife and partner in adventure, even today spurs the family forward with her vision and motivation, just as she has done for decades. And as we moved toward creating a narrative of the most significant events, her insight and comments have been invaluable.

Without my children, Cricket, David, Autumn, Forest, Rivers and Canyon, there would be no book. Published writers in their own right, their lives make up the substance of these pages. All have read manuscripts, made suggestions and contributed their own words to the text. An extra shout-out to Cricket, who brought the HeadwatersPublishing.com website up to speed and then completely reformatted the manuscript of this book and designed the cover for printing. Her heart and soul are in these pages!

Patch Adams has been close to our family's hearts for many years, his vision of medical care for all, regardless of resources, inspiring us to think in fresh directions. Few individuals are as familiar with so many people of the world, bringing laughter and healing to children and adults who never anticipated such an experience. Autumn and Rivers have traveled with him to Peru and Haiti, their service work bringing smiles to many faces. His words in the foreword of this book are a rare gift to us all.

Erin McKittrick, an Alaskan adventurer, as are her husband, Hig, and two small children, made an honest developmental edit of the manuscript, urging me to add and delete whole segments, as well as rearrange the timeline. She is an accomplished author of two books of her own, *A Long Trek Home* and *Small Feet, Big Land*, whose adventures will have you turning pages as you follow their young family into the wilds of Alaska in all seasons.

Alan Kesselheim and his wife, Marypat, are another pair of

intrepid North Country adventurers who have been an inspiration to our family. They have planned and carried out wild-country river odysseys that would have astounded the Voyageurs of old. Always including their three children in this way of life, the kids have been raised with adventure in their blood. Alan is a prolific author, his latest book, *Let Them Paddle*, taking the reader back to the "birth river" of each of their three children.

Ethan Hubbard, through his *Journey to Ollantaytambo*, a compelling account of his first time in Peru, dispelled our doubts and let us say, "Hey, that's something we can enjoy, too!" World traveler, superb photographer, and author of many other books, Ethan has that rare knack for capturing in his images the love and essence of each of his subjects. His love of life and the ability to "stay young" were never more apparent than when we shared a couple of days of wild sledding at his home in Vermont.

For several years, we have had, on our kitchen windowsill a postcard bearing Wade Davis's powerful words from his book, *One River*. An author of many first-hand accounts of indigenous people fighting for their very survival, Wade generously gave us permission to use his words at the end of the Choose Love, Not Fear chapter of this book.

When I wrote Forest's section, I had carefully selected his own words from a short speech he gave after the film Food Chains (of which he was photography director) debuted at New York's Tribeca Film Festival. Then *Sea Stoke* magazine appeared and I saw that Gary Parker's interview of Forest was perfect for the book. Thanks, Gary, for permission to use it here.

A big thanks to Kristina Moe and Erin Marsten for commenting on early manuscripts, to Cassie Chambliss for her research, Charles Diede and Stephan Findlay for their knowledge of Library of Congress cataloging, and to the staff of Fontana Regional Library for providing such a welcoming space in which to write. Pete Rathbun's eye for detail and his much appreciated professional editing skills have smoothed the text into a stream-lined reading experience.

Doug Woodward

Bringing with him expertise from another lifetime — working with teens to build boats in his basement workshop and planning odysseys to rivers of the West in an old school bus — Doug easily adapted these skills and his engineering background to family life on the mountain, as well as the adventures to which he and Trish would introduce their children.

He carries a deep love for the land on which he and Trish chose to build their family home. Located in a natural watershed, care of the water quality and the design of several gravity water systems have been priorities for Doug. He continues to enjoy planning and carrying out new projects, blending them with Nature's design, and can analyze and repair almost any problem that occurs in the house or on the mountain.

Doug is passionate when it comes to carving out time for writing, whether the project is a new book, a short story or a poem that is begging to be brought to life. His writing and photography have appeared in numerous outdoor magazines, from the U.S. to England and Germany.

If an environmental or social problem needs attention, you will likely find a letter from Doug to the appropriate congressman, as well as in the local newspapers.

Doug's award-winning book, *Wherever Waters Flow, A Lifelong Love Affair With Wild Rivers*, takes the reader on spine-tingling whitewater journeys as the author shares first-hand experiences from the filming of the movie *Deliverance* as well as challenging Chattooga River trips with Jimmy Carter.

Did you enjoy reading *You Took The Kids Where?* or feel that it helped give you the courage to take your kids into experiences that you hadn't previously considered possible?

Do you have friends or family wondering if they can continue an adventurous lifestyle as they start a family?

If so, a gift of *You Took The Kids Where?* could be just the motivation they need to open doors to adventure for both their children and themselves.

Copies of *You Took The Kids Where?* or the award-winning *Wherever Waters Flow* may be ordered online from Headwaters Publishing, at headwaterspublishing.com. Doug will be glad to autograph or inscribe copies of any books ordered in this manner.

HEADWATERS
PUBLISHING

HeadwatersPublishing.com